MARIE KONDO started reading housewives' magazines from the age of five and loved the order and beauty of the well-organized spaces she saw in them. Then, from the age of 15 she started studying tidying seriously. She started with her own bedroom and then moved on to her siblings'. Today she runs a highly successful business in Tokyo helping clients transform their cluttered homes into spaces of beauty, peace and inspiration. Her internationally bestselling publishing phenomenon *The Life-Changing Magic of Tidying* was first published in English in 2014. She lives in Tokyo with her husband and daughter.

# SPARK
# JOY

An Illustrated Guide
to the Japanese Art
of Tidying

MARIE KONDO

Vermilion
LONDON

7 9 10 8

Vermilion, an imprint of Ebury Publishing,
20 Vauxhall Bridge Road,
London SW1V 2SA

Vermilion is part of the Penguin Random House group of companies whose
addresses can be found at global.penguinrandomhouse.com

Illustrations Copyright © Masako Inoue

English translation by Cathy Hirano

Marie Kondo has asserted her right to be identified as the author of this Work in
accordance with the Copyright, Designs and Patents Act 1988

First published in the United Kingdom by Vermilion in 2016
First published in the United States by Ten Speed Press in 2016, an imprint of the
Crown Publishing Group, a division of Penguin Random House LLC, New York

Originally published in Japan in 2012 and 2015 with the titles *The Life-Changing
Magic of Tidying Up 2* and *The Illustrated Life-Changing Magic of Tidying Up* by
Sunmark Publishing Inc., Tokyo, Japan

English translation rights arranged with Sunmark Publishing, Inc., through
InterRights Inc,. Tokyo, Japan, and Gudovitz & Company, New York, USA

www.eburypublishing.co.uk

A CIP catalogue record for this book is available from the British Library

ISBN 9781785040481

Printed and bound in Italy by L.E.G.O. S.p.A.

Penguin Random House is committed to a
sustainable future for our business, our readers
and our planet. This book is made from Forest
Stewardship Council® certified paper.

# Contents

## Part I  KonMari master tips

# Part II The tidying encyclopaedia

## 8 Tidying sentimental items   221

# Part III  Life-changing magic

# Preface

L ife truly begins only after you have put your house in order. That's why I've devoted most of my life to the study of tidying. I want to help as many people as possible tidy up once and for all.

This doesn't mean, however, that you should just dump anything and everything. Far from it. Only when you know how to choose those things that spark joy can you attain your ideal lifestyle.

If you are confident that something brings you joy, keep it, regardless of what anyone else might say. Even if it isn't perfect, no matter how mundane it might be, when you use it with care and respect, you transform it into something priceless. As you repeat this selection process, you increase your sensitivity to joy. This not only accelerates your tidying pace but also hones your decision-making capacity in all areas of life. Taking good care of your things leads to taking good care of yourself.

**What sparks joy for you personally? And what doesn't?**

The answers to these questions represent a major clue for getting to know yourself as a recipient of the gift of life. And I am convinced that the perspective we gain through this process represents the driving force that can make not only our lifestyle, but our very lives, shine.

Some people have told me that they had almost nothing left after discarding those things that didn't spark joy and, at first, didn't know what to do. This reaction seems particularly common when people finish tidying their clothes. If it happens to you, don't be discouraged. The important thing is that you have noticed. The real tragedy is to live your entire life without anything that brings you joy and never even realize it. From the moment you finish tidying, you can begin to add a new zest to your home and to your life.

Only two skills are necessary to successfully put your house in order: the ability to keep what sparks joy and chuck the rest, and the ability to decide where to keep each thing you choose and always put it back in its place.

The important thing in tidying is not deciding what to discard but rather what you want to keep in your life. It is my hope that the magic of tidying will help you create a bright and joyful future.

# Introduction:
# The KonMari Method

'KonMari, is there an illustrated guide that explains your tidying methods the same way you do in your lessons?'

I don't know how many times I've been asked this question. My response has always been the same. 'But you don't need one, because success depends 90 per cent on your mind-set.' I know that no matter how much knowledge you may gather, if you don't change your way of thinking, you'll rebound. What I'm trying to share as a tidying consultant is not a mere tidying method but rather an approach that will enable you to become capable of tidying. And I believe that to achieve this, something similar to shock treatment is necessary.

At the same time, however, it's true that once people have committed themselves to tidying up, they may want more detailed instructions. For people in the middle of the tidying process, then, what could be more helpful than an illustrated guide? For people who have not yet committed themselves, however, such a book could actually make things worse. In that sense, publishing this illustrated guide could be likened to sharing a book of forbidden knowledge.

So, let me ask you point-blank: are you committed to completing the once-in-a-lifetime special event of tidying up? If you answered yes, then please go ahead and read this book. Even if you have already finished your tidying campaign, the tips for making your home spark joy are bound to be of use. If you answered no, however, please start by reading my first book, *The Life-Changing Magic of Tidying*. If you have already read it but still aren't committed, please read it again, because something, and probably something quite small, has kept you from tidying up so far.

This illustrated guide is a comprehensive compilation of KonMari Method know-how. For people who have made the commitment to tidy up once and for all, it should be extremely helpful, like a hand scratching your back right where you feel itchy, and I hope that you will read it from cover to cover. For those of you who have tidied up to some extent but want more details, this guide will serve as an 'Encyclopaedia of Tidying'. Feel free to skip to the relevant sections whenever you need to confirm how specific tasks are done. I've also included answers to many of the questions I received from readers of the first volume. And for those of you who want to skip all my personal stories and are impatient to get to the nitty-gritty of tidying, this book alone may be enough.

Now, are you ready? Don't forget that the 'god of tidying' is always on your side as long as you are committed to getting it done.

# The six basic rules of tidying

The tidying process you are about to embark on is not about decluttering your house or making it look neat on the spur of the moment for visitors. Rather, you are about to tidy up in a way that will spark joy in your life and change it forever.

When you tidy the KonMari way, you will experience several changes. For one thing, when you have finished cleaning up once and for all, you will never again relapse into clutter. You also will have clearly identified your values and what you want to do. You will be able to take good care of your possessions and will experience, every day, a feeling of contentment. The key to success is to tidy up quickly and completely, all in one go.

Once you have experienced what your house feels like when it is completely tidy in the true sense of the term, you will never want to return to clutter, and the strength of that feeling will empower you to keep it tidy.

## 1. Commit yourself to tidying up

The KonMari Method may seem a little hard. It does require time and effort. But, having picked up this book with the intention of at least making a good stab at seriously tidying up, please keep reading. And believe in yourself. Once you have made up your mind, all you need to do is to apply the right method.

## 2. Imagine your ideal lifestyle

Think about what kind of house you want to live in and how you want to live in it. In other words, describe your ideal lifestyle. If you like drawing, sketch out what it looks like. If you prefer to write, describe it in a notebook. You can also cut out photos from magazines.

You would rather start tidying right away, would you? That is precisely why so many people suffer rebound after tidying up. When you imagine your ideal lifestyle, you are actually clarifying why you want to tidy and identifying the kind of life you want to live once you have finished. The tidying process thus represents a huge turning point in a person's life. So seriously consider the ideal lifestyle to which you aspire.

## 3. Finish discarding first

One characteristic of people who never seem to finish tidying up is that they attempt to store everything without getting rid of anything. When things are put away, a home will look neat on the surface, but if the storage units are filled with unnecessary items, it will be impossible to keep them organized, and this will inevitably lead to a relapse.

The key to success in tidying is to finish discarding first. You can only plan where to store your things and what to store them in once you've decided what to keep and what to discard, because only then will you have an accurate grasp of how much actually needs to be stored.

Thinking about where to store things, or worrying about whether you can fit everything in, will only distract you from the job of discarding, and you will never finish. That would be a terrible waste; so instead, consider any storage solutions made during the discarding process as temporary and focus all your attention on sorting the next category. This is the secret to getting the job done quickly.

## 4. Tidy by category, not by location

One of the most common mistakes people make is to tidy room by room. This approach doesn't work because people think they have tidied up when in fact they have only shuffled their things around from one location to another or scattered items in the same category around the house, making it impossible to get an accurate grasp of the volume of things they actually own.

The correct approach is to tidy by category. This means tidying up all the things in the same category in one go. For example, when tidying the clothes category, the first step is to gather every item of clothing from the entire house in one spot. This allows you to see objectively exactly how much you have. Confronted with an enormous mound of clothes, you will also be forced to acknowledge how poorly you have been treating your possessions. It's very important to get an accurate grasp of the sheer volume for each category.

## 5. Follow the right order

It is crucial not only to tidy by category but also to follow the correct order, which is clothes, books, papers, *komono* (miscellany), and finally, sentimental items.

Have you ever run across old photos while tidying and found that hours have passed while you were looking at them? This is a very common blunder, and it clearly illustrates the point of tidying in the proper order, which is designed specifically to help you hone your ability to distinguish what sparks joy. Clothes are ideal for practising this skill, while photos and other sentimental items are the epitome of what you should not touch until you have perfected it.

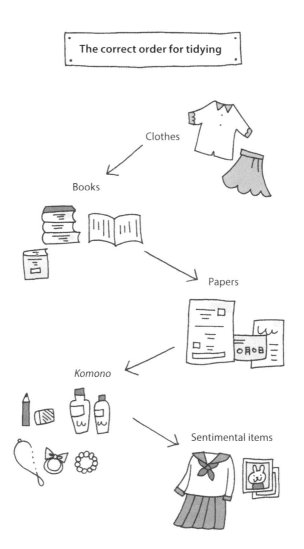

Clothes

Books

Papers

*Komono*

Sentimental items

## 6. Ask yourself if it sparks joy

The criterion for deciding what to keep and what to discard is whether or not something sparks joy. When deciding, it's important to touch it, and by that, I mean holding it firmly in both hands as if communing with it. Pay close attention to how your body responds when you do this. When something sparks joy, you should feel a little thrill, as if the cells in your body are slowly rising. When you hold something that doesn't bring you joy, however, you will notice that your body feels heavier.

Remember that you are not choosing what to discard but rather what to keep. Keep only those things that bring you joy. And when you discard anything that doesn't, don't forget to thank it before saying goodbye. By letting go of the things that have been in your life with a feeling of gratitude, you foster appreciation for, and a desire to take better care of, the things in your life.

## DON'T LEAVE TIDYING UP UNTIL AFTER MOVING

When people ask me whether it's best to tidy before or after moving, I always say, 'Before!' If you haven't even found a new house yet, then start tidying right away. Why? Because it's the house you live in now that will lead you to your next house.

I sometimes think that all houses must be connected by some kind of network. It's as if, when you tidy your house properly, your house announces to the network that you take good care of your home, and this attracts another one to you. At least, that's my conception of how it works.

Countless clients have told me that once they tidied up they found the perfect home, and the stories of how they discovered them are quite amazing. So if you want to meet a beautiful home that is just right for you, take good care of the one you live in now.

# PART I

# KonMari master tips

# 1

# Honing your sensitivity to joy

## Tidying is the act of confronting yourself; cleaning is the act of confronting nature

'This time I'm going to do it! I'm launching a year-end tidying marathon!'

In Japan, the year-end is traditionally the time to clean the whole house in preparation for the New Year (it's like 'spring cleaning' in some other countries). Every December, television programmes and magazine articles feature cleaning tips, and cleansers and other goods are prominently displayed in stores. People throw themselves into this year-end cleaning spree as if it were a national event, so that sometimes I think it must be programmed into the Japanese DNA.

When it is all over, however, it is amazing how many people say, 'I really tidied up at the end of the year, but I didn't manage to finish by New Year's.' When I ask them what they did, it becomes clear that almost all of them tidied as they cleaned. In other words, they randomly threw away whatever unnecessary items happened to catch their eye, wiped the floors and walls as they emerged beneath piles of stuff, donated boxes of books, wiped down the shelves on which those books had been sitting . . .

Let me be very clear. With this approach, you will spend the rest of your life tidying. It is only natural that such 'year-end cleaning' ends up half done. I will be honest. For years, my family and I used exactly the same approach, and we never once succeeded in making our house spick-and-span before the New Year.

The words *tidying* and *cleaning* are often used synonymously, but they are two completely different things. If you don't recognize this important truth, then your home will never be truly clean. First, the focus is different. Tidying deals with objects; cleaning deals with dirt. Both are aimed at making a room look clean, but tidying means moving objects and putting them away, while cleaning means wiping and sweeping away dirt.

The responsibility for mess and clutter lies 100 per cent with the individual. Things do not multiply of their own accord, but only if you buy them or receive them from someone else. Clutter accumulates when you fail to return objects to their designated place. If a room becomes cluttered 'before you know it', it is entirely your own doing. In other words, **tidying up means confronting yourself.**

In contrast, dirt does accumulate of its own accord. It is a law of nature that dust and dirt pile up. Therefore, **cleaning means confronting nature.** Cleaning must be done regularly to remove naturally accumulated dirt. This is precisely why Japan's year-end event is not called a 'tidying' spree but rather a 'cleaning' spree. If you want to succeed at year-end cleaning, the secret is to finish your tidying marathon beforehand.

In my previous book, I explain that a 'tidying marathon' means completing the process of discarding, thoroughly and quickly, and deciding where to store everything that you have chosen to keep. You only need to do this once. If you make up your mind and just get it done, you'll be able to truly concentrate on year-end cleaning. More often than not, people who think that they are not good at cleaning actually don't know how to tidy. My clients who have finished tidying up frequently say that cleaning now takes them no time at all. In fact, they like doing it, whereas before it made them feel totally incompetent.

Cleaning the temple is part of Buddhist training, but tidying the temple is not. With cleaning, we can let our minds empty while our hands keep moving, but tidying requires us to think – about what to discard, what to keep, and where to put it. **You could say that tidying orders the mind while cleaning purifies it.** If you want to clean your house for the New Year, then start with a tidying marathon. No matter how hard you try, your house will never be truly clean if you don't finish tidying first.

# If you don't know what brings you joy, start with things close to your heart

'I feel . . . uhm . . . joy . . . I, uh, I think I feel . . . joy . . . I feel . . . something between joy and . . . no joy.'

At her first lesson, my client sits frozen before a mountain of clothing. A white T-shirt is clutched in her hand, and a garbage bag lies ready to one side. She puts the T-shirt back on the pile and picks up the grey cardigan beside it. After staring at it for ten seconds, she slowly raises her eyes. 'I don't know what "joy" feels like,' she says finally.

As you know by now, the key to my approach is to keep only those things that spark joy and to discard the rest. **Does it spark joy when you touch it?** While some people find this criterion easy to grasp, many wonder what it actually means, and my clients are no exception. When that happens, I give them this exercise.

*Pick the top three items in this pile that give you joy. You have three minutes to decide.*

In the case described above, my client paused for a moment to think. 'The top three . . .' she muttered. Then she rummaged through the pile, pulled out five items, and spread them in a row. After rearranging them several times, she returned two of them to the pile, and, just when her time was up, announced firmly, 'These are the top three from right to left!' Before her lay a white dress with a green flower print, a beige mohair jumper and a blue flowered skirt.

'That's it!' I told her. 'That's joy!'

I was quite serious. **The best way to identify what does or doesn't bring you joy is to compare.** In the beginning, unless your feelings are very black-and-white, it's hard to decide if something brings joy when you look at it by itself. When you compare it with a bunch of other things, however, your feelings become clear. This is why it's so important to sort only one category at a time, starting with clothing.

This 'top-three' joy ranking method can be used for other categories as well. If you're stuck on books or hobby items, give it a try. As long as you stick to the same category, you'll find that you not only can identify the best three but will also be able to clearly rank everything. Of course, giving every individual item a rank would take a long time, but by the time you have chosen the top ten or twenty, you will see that anything below a certain rank has finished its usefulness. Discovering your personal 'joy line' is a fascinating process.

Let me share another special trick for identifying what gives you joy when you are just beginning to sort your clothes: start with the ones that you wear close to your heart. Can you guess why? Because that's where you feel joy – in your heart, not in your head. The closer your clothing is to your heart, the easier it is to choose. For example, bottoms, such as trousers and skirts, are easier than socks; tops, such as blouses and shirts, are easier than bottoms. Technically, lingerie, such as brassieres and camisoles, are worn closest to the heart, but most people don't have enough to make a proper comparison. Therefore, my rule of thumb is to start with your tops.

If you feel unsure about any piece of clothing, don't just touch it; hug it. The difference in how your body responds when you press it against your heart can help you recognize if it sparks joy. Try touching, hugging and gazing closely at any items about which you are not certain. As a last resort, you can even try them on. If you have many outfits you want to try on, it's more effective to put these in a separate pile and try them on in one go when you've finished sorting your other clothes.

It can be hard to recognize what brings you joy at first. One of my clients took as long as fifteen minutes to check the first piece of clothing she picked up. Even if you feel like it's taking you a long time, there's no need to worry. Differences in speed simply reflect differences in length of experience. If you take sufficient time to explore your own sense of joy at the beginning, the speed with which you make decisions will accelerate rapidly. So don't give up. If you keep trying, you, too, will soon reach that stage.

# 'It might come in handy' is taboo

One of my clients' top questions is 'What should I do about things that I need even though they don't spark joy?' Many people feel perplexed when deciding what to do with clothing items that are purely practical, such as long winter thermals that are only worn on the coldest days of the year. The same is true when they are trying to select tools, such as scissors or screwdrivers.

'This doesn't particularly thrill me, but I need it, don't I?' This is a common refrain, and my response is always this: **If it really doesn't spark joy, go ahead and dis- card it!** If, at that point, my client says, 'Hmm, why not? Let me dispose of it,' then that's fine. More commonly, however, they'll protest. 'No, wait. I need it,' or 'But I use it sometimes.' If so, I encourage them to keep it with confidence.

While this response may appear irresponsible, in fact, it's based on many years of experience. I began seriously studying the art of tidying when I was in junior high. After going through a phase where I discarded everything as if I were a machine, I discovered the importance of keeping only those things that spark joy, an approach I've been practising ever since. I have bid farewell, at least temporarily, to countless things that didn't bring me joy and, to be frank, the absence of a discarded item never caused a catastrophe. There was always something in the house that would serve as a substitute.

For example, one day I threw away a vase that was chipped, only to miss it the very next day. I made a perfect substitute, however, by covering a plastic bottle with a favourite piece of cloth. After discarding a hammer because the handle was worn out, I used my frying pan to pound in any nails. Since getting rid of my stereo speakers, which had sharp corners and simply didn't bring me any joy, I've used my headphones as speakers.

Of course, if I need something badly, I will buy another, but having come this far, I can no longer buy something just to make do. Instead, I consider the design, the feel, the convenience and every other factor important to me extremely carefully until I find one that I really love. And that means that the one I choose is the very best, something that I will cherish all my life.

Tidying up is far more than deciding what to keep and what to discard. Rather, it's a priceless opportunity for learning, one that allows you to reassess and fine-tune your relationship with your possessions and to create the lifestyle that brings you the most joy. Doesn't that make tidying up even more fun?

It may seem rather drastic, but I'm convinced that letting go, at least once, of anything that doesn't bring you joy is the ultimate way to experience what it's like to surround yourself only with things that do bring you joy.

*'It might come in handy.'* Believe me, it never will. You can always manage without it. For those embarked upon a tidying marathon, this phrase is taboo.

# For essential things that don't bring joy, look at what they do for you

As I just mentioned, I substituted a plastic bottle for a vase I threw out. It was light, unbreakable and required no storage space. I could simply recycle it when I no longer needed it. I could also cut it to the size I wanted and play with different designs by changing the cloth that covered it. Although I have since purchased a glass vase that I really like, I still use bottles when I have too many flowers for one vase.

Using my headphones as speakers was also a great solution for my simple lifestyle. I raised the volume loud enough to hear without wearing them. Music aficionados might shudder in horror, but for me the volume and sound quality were more than adequate for my room, and I was quite content. I cannot begin to count all the new pleasures I have discovered just by discarding.

Having said this, I must admit that there have been a few exceptions. Take, for example, my vacuum cleaner.

I got rid of it because it was an outdated model, and instead diligently wiped the floor with paper towels and rags. But in the end it simply took too much time, and I had to buy a new vacuum.

And then there was my screwdriver. After throwing it away, I tried using a ruler to tighten a loose screw, but it snapped down the middle. This almost reduced me to tears as it was one I really liked.

All these incidents stemmed from youthful inexperience and thoughtlessness. They demonstrated that I had not yet honed my ability to discern what brings me joy. Deceived by their plainness, I failed to realize that I actually liked them. I had assumed that if something brought me joy, I would feel a thrill of excitement that made my heart beat faster. Now I see things differently.

Feelings of fascination, excitement, or attraction are not the only indications of joy. **A simple design that puts you at ease, a high degree of functionality that makes life simpler, a sense of rightness, or the recognition that a possession is useful in our daily lives – these, too, indicate joy**.

If something clearly sparks no joy, then obviously we aren't going to agonize about discarding it. When we do feel torn about something, there are three possible reasons: the item once brought us joy but has fulfilled its purpose; it does bring us joy but we don't realize it; or we need to keep it regardless of whether or not it sparks joy. Included within the third possibility are contracts, formal outfits and mourning clothes, various items needed for weddings, funerals and other special occasions, and things that if discarded without permission could cause a back-lash from other people, such as family members.

**I have a secret for raising our joy level for things we know we need but that fail to excite us: shower them with praise.** Let them know that while they may not inspire joy, you really need them.

It might sound something like this.

'Hey! Look at you, slip. You're the best! Jet black and smooth as satin, you complement the line of my dress without ever stealing the show. What charming grace and elegance. Way to go!'

Or how about this?

'Dear old screwdriver, I may not use you much, but when I need you, why, you're a genius. Thanks to you, I put this shelf together in no time. You saved my finger-nails, too. I would have ruined them if I had used them to turn the screws. And what a design! Strong, vigorous and cool to the touch, with a modern air that makes you really stand out.'

While it may look somewhat pathetic on paper, a lit-tle exaggeration is much more fun. The point is this: the things we need definitely make our lives happier. **There-fore, we should treat them as things that bring us joy.** Through this process, we learn to accurately identify even those items that are purely utilitarian as things that bring us joy.

One theme of my regular lessons is appreciating every item we use. This is a highly effective way to hone our judgement. By the time my clients begin tackling such items as kitchen implements, they can declare quite confidently that an unremarkable frying pan or a plain old egg beater brings them joy. Or the opposite may occur. Some of my clients have discovered that none of their work clothes spark joy. When they explored the reason, they realized that it was their job that failed to thrill them. **Thus, while some items we assume don't spark joy actually do, sometimes the lack of that spark represents our own inner voice.** This shows how deep the bond is between us and our possessions.

As we hone our sense of what brings us joy through the process of tidying, we come to know ourselves far better. This is the ultimate purpose of tidying up.

## Save your 'cosplay' for indoors

'That dress brings me joy, but I know I'll never wear it again. I guess I'd better discard it, right?' my client said with obvious hesitation.

I followed the direction she was pointing and saw a vivid blue dress covered in flowers and trimmed with gold. The sleeves were puffed at the shoulders, and five tiers of ruffles adorned the skirt. She was right. It was a little too gaudy for regular use. She explained that she had worn it for performances when she took dance lessons. Even if she were to go back, however, she said there'd be no opportunity to wear it because she would want a new dress for performing.

'It always gives me a thrill when I look at it, but I should probably just get rid of it,' she said. Reluctantly, she reached for a garbage bag.

'Wait a minute!' I exclaimed. 'Why don't you keep it to wear around the house?'

She looked at me in surprise, then her expression grew serious. 'Wouldn't that be weird?' A very reasonable question.

'But it brings you joy, right?' I pressed her.

She paused for a few seconds, then said, 'Let me try it and see. In fact, I'll put it on right now!' She picked up the dress and went into the next room. Three minutes later the door opened, and she walked in, completely transformed. Gone were her casual jeans and T-shirt. She not only wore the blue dress, but had also donned gold earrings and a yellow flower hair ornament. She had even redone her makeup. This time, it was my turn to be surprised. Her transformation far surpassed my expectations. As I sat there speechless, she looked at herself in the mirror and smiled.

'It's not bad, is it? I think I'll wear this for the rest of our session!'

While this is an extreme example, a surprisingly high percentage of my clients have costume-like clothes. To name just a few, I have encountered a Chinese dress, a maid's outfit, and a belly-dancing costume. If the client loves it, parting with it can be very hard. If it brings you joy, but you can't see yourself wearing it outside, there's no reason you shouldn't wear it inside.

Even if you feel a bit embarrassed, I suggest that you at least try it. If you decide an outfit looks too ridiculous when you see yourself in the mirror, you can accept that it's time to get rid of it. And if it looks much better than you expected, enjoy it and add a taste of the extraordinary to ordinary life. Just be sure to warn your family first.

When you wear and surround yourself with the things you love, your house becomes your own personal paradise. Don't throw away things that bring you joy simply because you aren't using them. You could end up taking all the joy out of your home. Instead, get creative and find ways to utilize those seemingly useless things. Try plastering a wardrobe wall with photographs of your favourite musicians to create a custom-made 'joy corner'. Or cover the front of a plastic storage drawer with a stash of lovely postcards to conceal the drawer's contents. Thinking up ideas for how you *can* use the things you love makes tidying that much more fun.

# Don't confuse temporary clutter with rebound

'I'm so sorry. I've suffered a rebound.' I froze when I read the first line of my client's email.

'This is it,' I thought. 'It has finally happened.'

Ever since I began giving private lessons at my clients' homes, I have maintained a zero rebound rate. People sometimes laugh and say, 'You can't be serious. There's no way it could really be zero,' or 'How did you rig those figures?' But it really is true. This shouldn't be so surprising. Anyone who learns to tidy properly should never rebound.

'Oh dear,' I thought. 'I'll have to start saying that my method "used to have" a zero rebound rate. But first I'd better apologize and offer retraining.'

Anxiously, I checked the name of the sender and got another surprise. It was not from someone who had already 'graduated' from the course, but from a woman who still had the *komono* and sentimental item categories to go. Her final lesson was scheduled at the end of the month. Still, even in the middle of the course, no one had ever claimed before that they had suffered a rebound. Obviously, something must have happened. I knew that as a working mother with two young children, she must be overwhelmingly busy, and that her husband, who also worked full-time, would not have much time to help her.

When I went to our final session, she apologized yet again. 'I'm really sorry. Things are back to the way they were at our first lesson.' Clothes were piled in a corner of the living room, the tatami-mat room was strewn with toys, and dishes were stacked on the kitchen counter. She was in no state for a lesson.

'Let's at least put away the things for which you have assigned a storage space.'

'Good idea. You know, I managed to tidy up my desk at work quite a bit, too,' she said. We chatted about this and that while she returned everything to its proper place. She folded the clothes and returned them to their drawers in the wardrobe, then put the toys in a plastic box, the stuffed toy animals in a rattan basket, and the papers her kids had been playing with in the recycle bin. Spices went back into the kitchen rack, and the clean dishes went into the cupboard. Within thirty minutes, her house was back to the state it had been at our last lesson, with nothing left on the table or the floor.

'You see, I can get it clean like this in just thirty minutes,' she said. 'But when I'm busy, I tend to leave things out. I rebound like this two or three times a month.'

In fact, this does not count as a rebound. This is just temporary clutter caused by not putting things back in their place on a daily basis. Rebound and clutter are quite different. Rebound means the state where things without a designated storage place begin inundating your home all over again, even though you tidied up completely, once and for all. As long as everything has a place where it belongs, a certain amount of clutter is not a problem.

I must confess that when work gets really busy, I rush out the door in the morning and come home exhausted in the evening. Before I know it, laundry waiting to be folded piles up. But I don't panic because I know that when I have time, I can return my space to its proper state quickly and easily. It's a tremendous relief to know that I can tidy up in just thirty minutes.

Never assume you're on a rebound. Just the thought could kill your motivation and actually cause one. If you experience some clutter during your tidying marathon, don't be discouraged. Put things back in their designated spots whenever you can and carry on. (Remember: storage won't be finalized until the marathon is over, so just put things away where you've tentatively decided they belong.) The further along you get, the less time it will take you, so, really, there's no need to worry.

The key is to return to basics. Only when everything has been given its own place will you have reached your final goal. Stick with it, confident that you'll never rebound once you reach the finish line.

## When you feel like quitting

Have you started your tidying marathon only to find yourself sitting numbly in the middle of your room with no end in sight? Don't worry. Almost everyone experiences this feeling in the beginning.

Occasionally, one of my clients or students will exclaim, 'KonMari, I feel like quitting. I just got started on my clothes, but it's taking forever.' **Anxiety arises from not being able to see the whole picture.** If this happens to you, try making an inventory of your storage space. Step back and look at it objectively. Draw up a floorplan, make sketches, or write a list of what shelves and storage units are in the house and what kinds of things each contains. Things will inevitably turn up where you least expect once you get back to tidying, so you don't need to make a detailed record. Just aim for a general grasp of what categories of things are kept where.

When I go to someone's house for the first time, I don't leap right into sorting clothes. Instead, I start by checking all the storage space. Over and over again, I'll ask, 'What's in here? Do you keep things in this category anywhere else?' I make mental notes of the location and volume of every storage space, estimate how long the tidying process will take, and visualize the end result, including where everything will be kept.

But that's what I do as an instructor. Your purpose is simply to get an overview of the current state and regain your equilibrium. Don't spend too long on it. Ten to thirty minutes should be sufficient.

The process of taking stock actually gives you a little break. The simple act of listing each storage space in your house restores your objectivity. If you suddenly realize in the middle that this is no time to be taking stock, feel free to get back to tidying. If making an inventory becomes burdensome and actually interferes with the tidying process, then reset your priorities.

On the other hand, if you love taking notes and keeping records, be as thorough as you like. You could even make a checklist of the content of each storage unit. One of my clients went so far as to make a tidying journal. The first page presented her 'Ideal Lifestyle'. This was followed by a section called 'Current Situation (Tidying Problems, Storage Units, List of Things by Category)'. The last section was a progress sheet titled 'The Tidying Process', in which she recorded everything from the discoveries she made about tidying to the number of garbage bags she used.

'I love it when I successfully complete another category and see my list full of check marks,' she told me. If making a list gives you this much joy, feel free to take as much time as you need. And, while you're at it, why not think up other ways to enhance the joy you feel when tidying?

## The clutter-photo shock treatment

My first lesson with T was coming up in a week when I received the following email. She had already grasped the basics of how to tidy, had envisioned her ideal lifestyle, and had seemed all fired up to start, but now her enthusiasm appeared to have plummeted.

'I'm just so discouraged by the mess that I don't feel like having a tidying festival,' she wrote. 'I just can't get motivated . . .' She went on to list the hurdles in her way, such as, 'One of our rooms has become a storage shed, and my two kids keep undoing what I've done.' She topped it all off with, 'I'll never be able to tidy anyway because I'm blood type B.' (In Japan, there's a widespread belief that blood type influences personality, and type As are thought to have a stronger desire for neatness and order than type Bs.)

While I might be tempted to say, 'Quit complaining and get to work,' I know complaining is actually proof that a person still has the energy to carry on. The trick is to turn the current mess, which will soon be gone for good, into a source of entertainment.

How? By taking photos while each room is still a mess. That's right. I encourage you to click away, taking panoramas of each room in its entirety as well as close-ups of the contents of each drawer. A look at these photos will likely show you that your place is even messier than you thought. There may be piles of laundry and papers scattered about, or things that make you wonder how they even got there. This objective look at the reality of your space can be quite a shock, throwing you into despair.

But why would I want to rub it in and make you

feel even worse? Believe me, I'm not trying to be mean. I know exactly how hard it is to get motivated when you don't feel like doing something. It's just that, in my experience, it's more effective to hit rock bottom, rather than to push myself to try harder. Once I'm down there, I get fed up with being discouraged and can pick myself up much faster.

This method works well not only before you start tidying but also if you start to feel burned out midway. Enjoy your pictures to the full. Share them with your friends for a laugh as you compare your house before and after your tidying marathon. As your house becomes tidier, it's easy to forget what it was like when it was messy. A look at the photos will show you just how far you've come and encourage you to keep going. When my clients look at their photos after they've finished tidying up, they all exclaim, 'Whose messy house is that?'

# No matter how cluttered it looks, don't pause, don't stop, don't quit

Many years have passed since my first job in this field. I have seen so many cluttered homes that the messes I come across, no matter how bad, rarely faze me. Three or four heaps of clothing on the floor is normal. When a deluge of paper, ankle-deep, bursts from a room as I open the door, when all that can be seen inside are stacks of cardboard boxes, I'm ready to take it on. Yet when I arrived at K's house, the sight sent my head spinning, and I was sure that I had stepped into a demon's den.

The ground floor of K's house was her office, while the first and second floors were her residence. We passed through the office hallway, which seemed relatively empty, and climbed the stairs. When the door to her living quarters opened, however, I felt like I was entering the Twilight Zone.

A kitty litter box lay at my feet just inside the doorway. Pellets of what looked like cat kibble were strewn across the floor, making it difficult to navigate without stepping on them. I promptly crushed one the size of a coffee bean under my foot. Just as I was wondering what to do about the crumbs on my shoe, I glanced up, and all thoughts of kibble-crunch vanished from my mind.

The staircase before me was made of books. Or, to be more accurate, books, three or four deep, were stacked on every stair so that the wooden steps were no longer visible. Ignoring my speechless state, K said, 'I have so many books. The shed on the roof is literally bursting with them.' As she spoke, she sprang lightly up the steps like a steeplejack, despite the fact that the books looked as though they might slip out from under her floppy slippers at any moment. I, on the other hand, clung to the railing and climbed up gingerly, one step at a time, sure that if I fell, my head would land right in the kitty litter box. I couldn't help thinking this particular arrangement would make a great booby trap to deter would-be burglars.

I managed to reach the first floor in one piece and to pass poker-faced through the living room, in which an entire wall appeared to be made of books. K's bedroom was literally a cave of clothes. Clothes hanging from poles covered both sides of the room, narrowing the field of vision and obscuring the light.

K's lessons, of which this was the first, are still continuing. To be honest, it's taking quite a long time, and she will easily surpass the longest record of any of my clients. But her home has already been transformed into a new world compared to when she started. An art lover, K attends exhibits three or more times a month. While tidying, she has uncovered many beautiful ceramic works as well as prints of famous paintings. As the amount of clutter has decreased and the walls have re-emerged, she has begun hanging the prints for display. Works by Monet and Renoir bedeck one corner of her room, transforming it into a unique gallery. Gone is any trace of the demon's den it used to be.

Even so, K occasionally asks me, 'I know the places I've finished are still tidy, but are you sure it's okay to take so much time?'

My response is an emphatic 'Yes!' because the tidying process is definitely moving forward.

No matter how messy your house may be, tidying deals with physical objects. **No matter how much**

**stuff you may own, the amount is always finite.** If you can identify the things that bring you joy and decide where to keep them, the job of tidying must inevitably come to an end. The more you do it, the closer you get to a house full of joy. Therefore, nothing could be more wasteful than to give up in the middle.

Once you take the first step in your tidying marathon, don't pause, don't stop and don't quit. No matter what your current situation is, you can make your home a place that brings you joy. I guarantee it, because **tidying never lies.** The opposite is also true. If you don't keep at it, your tidying marathon will never end. So if you've stopped in the middle, stop procrastinating. It's time to get back to work.

# If you're terrible at tidying, you'll experience the most dramatic change

Before we start, I ask my clients, 'Are you good or bad at tidying?' I usually get one of three answers: good, not bad, or terrible. The ratio is approximately 1 to 3 to 6.

People who reply that they are good at it usually have fairly tidy homes already. Their questions tend to be extremely concrete because they've already tried out different methods. I simply respond to specific questions, such as, 'Is it better to keep the vacuum cleaner in the closet or in the storage room?' and 'I keep the towels here in the bathroom. Do you think this is all right?' They are also good at choosing what brings them joy, and the work moves along quite quickly. Often they just need help revising their storage and then we're finished.

People who are not bad at tidying are at least doing it in their own fashion and could carry on without any problem. Since they are trying so hard, however, it seems a waste not to make those efforts more effective. While they may have assigned places to keep their possessions, they still have many things that don't bring them joy, and their storage tends to be quite complex with items from the same category scattered throughout the house. My lessons take such people through the basics.

Finally, there are those who are terrible at tidying. Their marathon begins for the first time when I step through their door. When I see the amount of stuff strewn about, I sometimes wonder if they made all that mess on purpose just to entertain me, knowing that I'm a tidying freak. One client revealed that she thought her room was just there for storing things. More often than not, before these clients can even begin to tackle the 'joy check', we have to clear a space on the floor and vacuum it so that we can pile all the clothes in one spot.

Regardless of whether a client is good or bad at tidying, he or she can always learn to tidy up. But those who believe they're utterly hopeless at it are the ones who undergo the most dramatic transformation. Once they learn how, they continue to tidy with incredible faith-fulness. Personal perceptions of one's tidying skills are, in the end, just biased assumptions. People who see them-selves as bad at tidying have simply never known the right way to do it and therefore have never experienced what it's like to have a tidy house.

I once received an email from the husband of one of my clients, saying that his wife 'seems like a different per-son'. She used to be the type who never really noticed things, in both the good sense and the bad. 'She didn't look down, never turned around, never put anything back when she took it out. It didn't bother her at all. I used to be the one who did all the tidying, but now, she's like a different person, she's so diligent about tidying up.'

Imagine the impact such a change can have on your life. **The 'god of tidying' never abandons anyone, even those who don't believe in themselves.** But first, you have to decide to start. We can only transform our lives if we sincerely want to. And when we finish, the god of tidying is sure to reward us.

# 2

# How to fill your home with joy

## Imagine your perfect lifestyle from a single photograph

'Finish discarding first.' I'm sure you know by now that this is a cardinal rule of the KonMari Method. If you start thinking about where to store this and that before you have completely finished throwing stuff away, you won't get very far. That's why it's imperative to concentrate solely on discarding first.

Those of you who have already begun your tidying marathon know that, while you may start off rather hesitantly, once you get going, discarding is fun. This, however, is a warning bell. Just because it feels good is no reason to become a discarding machine. **The act of discarding things on its own will never bring joy to your life.**

Discarding is not the point; what matters is keeping those things that bring you joy. If you discard everything until you have nothing left but an empty house, I don't think you'll be happy living there. Our goal in tidying should be to create a living environment filled with the things we love.

That is also why it is so important to begin the whole process by identifying what you consider to be the ideal lifestyle. Concerning this, I have a request. Please don't curb your dreams. Your ideal image is not an objective set in stone nor is it an obligation, so don't hold back. Feel free to indulge your wildest fantasy. Do you want to live like a princess in a room with snow white furniture and bedcovers? Do you want a rich and gorgeous space with beautiful paintings on the wall? Or perhaps you want a room so filled with plants that you feel like you're living in a forest.

Having said that, some of you may find it hard to identify the lifestyle you want. In that case, I suggest searching for a single image that represents your ideal. Of course, you could just picture it in your mind, but if you have even one photograph that makes you feel, 'Yes, this is the kind of space I want to live in,' it will completely change how you feel about tidying up.

When looking for such an image, however, it's important to do so thoroughly and quickly, all in one go. If you are thinking, 'I'm bound to come across a photo at some point, so I'll just wait until I do,' it will never happen. The trick is to spread out multiple interior decorating magazines in front of you and look at them all at the same time. While it might be fun to look at a different magazine each day, if you proceed like that, you run the risk of being unable to make up your mind. Your opinion may change daily, making it even harder to identify the lifestyle you personally want. The interiors shown in magazines are all going to look fabulous. You'll be drawn to Japanese-style interiors one day and resort-style interiors the next. It's easier to identify what aspects of each you are drawn to if you look at a variety of interiors all at once. For example, you may notice that you tend to respond to white rooms, or that you are drawn to rooms with plants rather than any particular style.

Borrow a stack of interior decorating magazines from the library or buy them from the bookstore and flip through them quickly. When you find an image that speaks to you, keep it in your datebook or out on your desk so that you can refer to it all the time.

# Keep items in the grey zone with confidence

Tidying experts often recommend putting items we aren't sure about in a separate box. If they haven't been used after three months, they can be discarded. This sounds like a great idea and so easy, too. In the KonMari Method, however, I advocate doing the exact opposite, probably because this approach didn't work for me at all, despite two and a half years of trying.

When I first encountered it, it struck me not only as very simple and logical but also as a great excuse to discard things. 'Oh well, I didn't use it for three months, so I suppose it can't be helped.' At the time, I had become so obsessed with tidying that even I was beginning to feel that I was casting off too many things, and so the logic of this method dovetailed perfectly with my nebulous sense of guilt. Perhaps that's why I managed to stick with it for two and a half years, an unusual feat for me.

The first step was to put everything that fell into the grey zone, that is, everything that didn't thrill me, into a paper bag and store it on the floor inside my wardrobe on the right-hand side. I was supposed to label each item with the date of the 'judgement day', but I skipped that part as I didn't have that much stuff. For the next three months, life went on as usual.

I never used what I had put in that bag. In theory, whatever went in was being saved from the fate of being scrapped. This should have made me happy, but in fact I suffered a pang of conscience every time I saw it. I had organized the clothes in my wardrobe to flow upward to the right, which should have lifted my spirits, but the sight of that bag sucked my heart straight down. I thought it might help to move it to the left, but nothing changed.

I retrieved a bamboo paper knife someone had given me as a souvenir and began opening my letters with it, even though I really didn't need it. I took out a memo pad with cartoon characters on it that I had bought by mistake and didn't even like, but I only managed to use it once or twice. I already had more memo pads than I could ever use that I actually liked. All this because I kept thinking, 'Judgement day is coming soon.' Before long, I couldn't wait to get those three months over with. As the day finally approached, I began berating myself for not using the things in the bag. In the end, I felt three times guiltier when I disposed of those things than when I had first put them in the bag. The last time I put things in, I forgot about them completely for half a year.

Having gone through this experience, I would love to be able to sit down with my former self and give her some advice. 'Listen here,' I'd tell her. 'If you just can't bring yourself to discard something, then keep it without any guilt. You don't need to put things in a separate bag.' Instead of waiting to see if you'll use something in the next three months, why not just look back on the past three months and decide right now?

Try seeing it from the perspective of the things in that bag. Essentially, you've told them, 'You know, you don't particularly thrill me and I doubt I'll ever use you again, but just stay put here for three months.' Having rejected and segregated them, you then subject them to the humiliation of being told three months later, 'Hmm, just as I thought. You don't thrill me,' and getting rid of them anyway. This must be pure torture.

In my book, it's a crime to put things in detention so that we can justify throwing them away. To set them aside is to let ourselves hang on to things that don't bring us joy. **There are only two choices: keep it or chuck it. And if you're going to keep it, make sure to take care of it.**

When you decide to keep something that falls into the grey zone, treat it as though it were precious rather than giving it a half-hearted three-month grace period. This will free you from any feelings of guilt or ambivalence. Put it where you can see it so that you won't forget its existence. You might decide, for example, that you're going to part with something if you don't use it during the summer, but even so, while it is in your house, treat it with gratitude, as if it were something that you love. If, in the end, you realize that it no longer brings you joy and has served its purpose, thank it for all it has done and dispose of it.

Just to be clear, let me repeat. **Rather than hiding things that fall into the grey zone, keep them openly and willingly.** Treasure them just like you would anything else that sparks joy.

# A joy-filled home is like your own personal art museum

Having spent most of my life looking at things of every description, including those in my clients' homes, I have discovered three common elements involved in attraction: the actual beauty of the object itself (innate attraction), the amount of love that has been poured into it (acquired attraction), and the amount of history or significance it has accrued (experiential value).

While I have very few interests other than tidying, I do love spending time in art museums. I enjoy looking at paintings and photographs, too, but my favourite exhibits are of implements from daily life, such as dishes and urns. I believe that being appreciated by so many people refines and enhances such works of art and craft beyond their actual value. Sometimes I see a work in a museum that appears quite ordinary yet has a compelling attraction. In most cases, I expect this magnetic pull results from having been cherished by its owners.

I stumble across things with this same mysterious attraction in my clients' homes as well. N, for example, lived in an elegant house that had been her family's home for four generations, and it had a lot of dishes. The cabinet in the dining room and the dish cupboards in the kitchen were filled with them, and there were still more packed away in boxes in the storage room. When we had gathered them all up and placed them on the floor, they covered about three tatami mats (about six by nine feet of floor space). By this time, N was almost finished tidying the *komono* (miscellaneous) category, and she was quite proficient at checking. For a while, all that could be heard was the clink of dishes as she picked them up and put them down again, and the murmur of her voice as she said, 'This plate sparks joy. This cup doesn't.'

During this process, I usually keep my eyes on the objects in my clients' hands while pondering how to organize the storage. Suddenly, however, my eye was caught by a single small plate in the 'joy' corner. 'That plate is very special, isn't it?' I said.

N looked at me in surprise. 'No, not particularly. To tell you the truth, I'd even forgotten that I had it. I don't particularly like the design either, but something about it seemed to touch me.' A bit chunky and plain grey with no ornamentation, it did seem out of place among the other dishes she had chosen, most of which had colourful patterns.

After the lesson, she sent me an email telling me that she had asked her mother about it. Apparently, N's grandfather had made the little plate for his wife, N's grandmother, who had treasured it to the end of her life. 'It's so strange,' N wrote. 'Even though I had never heard that story, it still sparked joy.' She went on to relate several episodes concerning the plate. The next time I went to her house, it had been placed on the Buddhist altar to hold sweets, and the warmth it imparted to that space and its surroundings left a deep impression on me.

I'm convinced that things that have been loved and cherished acquire elegance and character. When we surround ourselves only with things that spark joy and shower them with love, we can transform our home into a space filled with precious artefacts, our very own art museum.

# Add colour to your life

'I've finished tidying up, and my place is lovely and clean! But somehow I don't feel like I'm actually done.' The homes of people who feel this way usually have one point in common: they lack colour.

Once the reducing phase is over, it's time to add joy. Normally, we can do this simply by decorating our space with things we love yet could not fully utilize before. But people who have very limited experience in choosing things that spark joy will have to search for them. Overwhelmingly, the one thing most often lacking in their lives is colour. While the ideal solution would be to buy new curtains or bedspreads in one's favourite colours or to put up a painting that one likes, this may not be an immediate option for everyone.

In such cases, the easiest solution is to use flowers. If you find cut flowers difficult to arrange, then potted plants are good, too. I began using flowers to brighten my room when I was a high school student. Or, to be exact, I used a single gerbera, which only cost a hundred yen, or about a dollar.

I used to wonder why colour seemed so important to me, but one day it hit me that it stems from the meals my mother used to cook. She always made a variety of dishes for each meal, and the result was very colourful. If there was too much of one colour, for example, stewed chicken and burdock, sautéed pork and mushrooms eggplant miso soup, and chilled tofu with a seaweed vinaigrette on top, she would look at the table and say, 'Too much brown. It needs more colour,' and then add a dish of sliced tomatoes. Surprisingly, that one touch brightened up the table and made our meal much more enjoyable. Our homes are the same. If a room looks bare, a single flower can cheer it up.

I once visited a celebrity's house to give a lesson for a TV programme. She lived in a duplex apartment with her workplace on the floor above her living quarters. Her workroom was comparatively neat and tidy, with only one cardboard box of documents sitting on the floor. After a quick check, we went downstairs to her bedroom and entered a shockingly different world.

The first thing that leaped into my eyes were six pin-ball-style slot machines displayed on top of a bookcase against one wall. The panels, bedecked with cartoon characters, flashed on and off, and the room was filled with the whir of machinery. While I have met people with dartboards and mah-jongg tables, I had never seen a home decorated with working slot machines. There were even two more sitting dormant on the wardrobe floor.

'These bring me the most joy of all!' she explained, grinning with confidence. Slot machines for her are like flowers for me, I thought, only even more so! When we had finished tidying up, the flashing machines were arranged prominently around her room, which must have seemed like a joy-filled paradise to her.

**It's far more important to adorn your home with the things you love than to keep it so bare it lacks anything that brings you joy.** When the tidying marathon ends, the homes of many of my clients often look quite empty, but they change and evolve quickly. A year later, the joy is clear to see. The things they love are displayed prominently, and often the curtains and bedspreads have been changed to their favourite colours. If you think that tidying up just means getting rid of clutter, you're wrong. Always keep in mind that the true purpose is to find and keep the things you truly love, to display these proudly in your home, and to live a joyful life.

# How to make the most of 'useless' things that still spark joy

' I 'm not sure this will be of any use. But just looking at it makes me happy. It's enough just to have it!' Usually a client will say this while holding up some random item that seems to have no conceivable purpose, such as a scrap of cloth or a broken brooch.

**If it makes you happy, then the right choice is to keep it confidently, regardless of what anyone else says.** Even if you keep it in a box, you'll still enjoy taking it out to look at it. But if you're going to keep it anyway, then why not get the most out of it? Things that seem senseless to others, things that only you could ever love – these are precisely the things you should display.

In general, there are four ways to use such items for decorating your home: place them on something (miniatures, stuffed animals, etc.); hang them (keychains, hair ties, etc.); pin or paste them up (postcards, wrapping paper, etc.); or use them as wraps or covers (anything pliable like scraps of cloth, towels, etc.).

Let's start with the first category – items to place on something. While this is pretty straightforward, it can be applied not only to things like ornaments and figurines, which were meant to be displayed in this way, but also to other items. A heap of them placed directly on top of a shelf can look rather messy, so I suggest 'framing' them by placing them together on a plate, a tray, a pretty cloth, or in a basket. This not only looks neater but is also easier to clean. Of course, if you actually prefer the more casual look of piling them directly on a shelf, please go ahead. Or use a display case if you have one.

In addition to displaying them in plain sight, it's also fun to put them in your storage spaces. One of my clients, for example, took a large corsage and stuck a rhinestone frog brooch in the centre so that the frog's face poked out. She then put this in a space between her brassieres inside a drawer. I'll never forget the smile on her face when she told me, 'It makes me happy just to see his face peeping out whenever I open this drawer.'

For the second category, items that hang, you can use

keychains or hair ties as accents in your clothes wardrobe by slipping them over the crooks of your hangers. You can also wrap the necks of hangers with longer things, such as gift-box ribbons or a necklace that you're tired of wearing. Or you can hang things from wall hooks, the ends of curtain rails, and anywhere else that looks feasible. If the item is too long and awkward-looking, you can cut it or tie it to adjust the length.

If you have so many things to hang that you run out of places, try stringing them together to make a single ornament. One of my clients made a curtain by stringing together cell phone straps of a local mascot she loved, and hung it across the entranceway. While the sight of the mascots' faces waving in the air looked rather bizarre, the owner declared that it transformed her doorway into 'the entrance to paradise'.

This brings us to the third category, items for pasting and pinning up. Decorating the inside of your wardrobe with posters you have no other place for is standard practice in the KonMari Method. This can inject a thrill into any kind of storage space, including your cupboard walls and wardrobe doors, the back boards of your shelves, and the bottoms of your drawers. You can use cloth, paper, or anything else, as long as it brings you joy.

Recently, I have noticed that many of my clients are making personalized bulletin boards with pictures of things that inspire them, such as samples of perfect homes or photos of countries they want to visit. These are like a collage of items that bring them joy. If you're interested, take the time to make one you really like.

The final category for decorating your interior with favourite items is things that can be used for wrapping. This includes anything supple, such as leftover scraps of cloth, hand towels, tote bags, and clothes made with beautiful patterns and fabrics that you love but that don't fit you any more. Such items can be used to bundle up cables that are long and unsightly or as dust covers for household appliances when they're not in use, such as electric fans in winter. Down quilts that are stored away for the off-season can be rolled up to expel the air inside and kept in a cloth carrying bag. This works just as well as vacuum-sealed storage bags.

If you enjoy sewing, you can make a great wrapper by undoing the seams of clothes and loop stitching the edges to keep them from unravelling. Simply bundling things in a pretty patterned cloth like this can create a beautiful space.

**By the time you finish, you'll see something you love everywhere you look.** When you open a drawer or the wardrobe, when you look behind your door or in the back of your shelves, your heart will overflow with joy. It may seem like an impossible dream, but it's within your grasp right now. If you have miscellaneous items that you love even though they seem useless, please give them a turn in the spotlight. There must have been a reason that you chose to bring them home with you in

## Add more spark to your storage

Place things

Hang things

Pin or
paste things

Wrap things

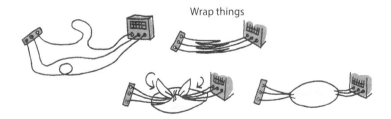

the first place. I'm quite sure that everything longs to be of use to its owner.

Incidentally, when you come across miscellaneous items that spark joy but seem useless during the tidying process, I recommend setting them aside in the 'decoration' category until you are finished. While you could stop to decorate each time you find one, if any decision making is involved, it can interrupt the tidying process. Decorating inspirations seem to pour forth once the tidying marathon is over, the home is clear and orderly and joy is at its height.

## Make your own personal power spot

One of my clients tidied up a small storage room and transformed it into her own personal space. She furnished it with a small, comfy sofa that wasn't being used, made a low bookcase by sawing off part of an old set of shelves, covered the walls in cloth that she loved instead of wallpaper, and used Christmas decorations to make a chandelier-style lamp. She did all of this herself. It took her three months, but the result was a lovely hideaway. Whenever her grandchildren come, they go into that room and never come out. 'It makes me feel so happy to spend time in here reading books or listening to music,' she told me.

Be sure to make a place in your home that is just for

you, your own personal space filled only with the things you love. If you don't have a whole room to yourself, use part of your wardrobe. If you have your own desk, this can become your personal space. If you are a stay-at-home parent who spends a lot of time in the kitchen, make a corner of the kitchen a space that sparks joy. One of my clients, for example, put up a corkboard displaying photos of her children, their handprints, and Mother's Day presents. 'I enjoy cooking much more than before,' she told me with obvious satisfaction.

The effects of making your own personal space, regardless of its location or size, are immeasurable. Having a place of your very own that is filled with joy is like having a hand warmer in your pocket on a freezing cold day.

One of my clients loved mushroom motifs. She had vivid mushroom postcards, mushroom figurines, keychains with little mushrooms dangling from them, an ear pick with a mushroom on the handle, and mushroom-shaped rubbers. 'It's the form that's so attractive, you see. Bulging on top and slender on the bottom. And their modesty; they flourish in the shade of great trees.' Her expression was rapturous as she described all their charms, and it was wonderful to see how much joy they brought her, but unfortunately, they were stored out of sight. Her mushroom cards remained in their plastic wrappers, the miniatures were still in their packages, and all were shoved casually into a large tin box that had once been filled with crackers.

When I asked her how often she opened the tin to look at them, she said once a month. So even if she spent two hours looking at them each time, she would only get twenty-four hours of joy from them in a whole year. At this rate, her precious mushrooms were going to grow mould. This is precisely the time to make your 'personal space' and use the things you love to decorate it to your heart's content.

This particular client created her own personal mushroom space inside her wardrobe. She decorated the fronts of her clear plastic storage boxes with mushroom postcards, covered the spare bedding with a large mushroom-patterned cloth, hung her mushroom keychains around the necks of her hangers, and displayed her mushroom miniatures in a basket on one of the shelves.

Imagine what it would be like to come home after a long, tiring day at work to your very own power spot. If you have reduced your possessions but feel no joy at home, try gathering selected items that you really love in one spot to create your own special space. This should dramatically increase the enjoyment you feel when you spend time at home.

# 3

# Everything you need to know about storing joyfully

## During the tidying process, storage is temporary

Just when tidying seems to be proceeding smoothly, you're suddenly overwhelmed with anxiety. You've drastically reduced the volume of things you own but haven't yet decided where to put what's left; and not only that, but the room looks like it is getting cluttered again. Could it be your imagination?

No, and those feelings aren't your imagination either. Many people experience the same thing, particularly when they've finished their clothes and books and are in the middle of doing the 'joy check' on their *komono* (miscellaneous items). For years, I, too, was worried about the same thing. But you can rest at ease. It is only natural for a room to get messy in the midst of a tidying marathon. The *komono* category, in particular, covers a broad spectrum of items and therefore causes quite a bit of clutter before you finish.

In the past, I once insisted that my clients decide where to store items as soon as they finished each *komono* category. 'Stationery goods into this drawer here, please,' 'Tools into that storage room there when you're done,' and so on. Storing things made the room look tidy right away, and, more importantly, it made me look professional. That's right, I was trying to show off.

But it's extremely difficult to get a proper grasp of your *komono* until you have sorted all of it. The number of categories is so extensive and what people own differs greatly from one individual to the next. To compound the matter, clients often classify things differently. To one person a box cutter may fall under 'stationery supplies' while to another it may fall under 'crafts'. People may also expand or revise the content of a category as they go along. 'Maybe this pocket hand warmer actually belongs under "medical supplies".'

When I had my clients store things as they tidied, neatly organized drawers soon began to overflow, and storage for items in the same category ended up scattered around the house. I would start to panic and my mind would go blank. In the end, I often had to say, 'I'm sorry, but do you mind if I take out the *komono* we just put away and have another look?' Then I'd have to start re-sorting the categories. Instead of saving them time, I had wasted it.

After repeating this mistake a few times, I finally realized that storage only falls into place at the very end. Only when you have finished sorting everything can you truly grasp how much you really have and identify the appropriate categories. Therefore, all storage should be considered temporary until you finish.

An important point during this process is to keep everything in one category, be it stationery goods or medical supplies, in a boxlike container rather than in paper or plastic bags where you won't be able to see what you have decided to keep. This will give you a better idea of how much you have left.

Once you have finished the 'joy check' for all of your *komono*, all you need to do is decide the place to store each category. You may have so much stuff that you can't sort through it in one day. In that case, it's no problem if you put the boxes in the cupboard for the time being to make room for your life.

If you end up with surplus plastic storage boxes while you're tidying, the rule of thumb is to set these aside, not get rid of them. Put them in a spot designated for storage items and use them at the end to 'balance accounts' for things that need storing. Of course, if you have discarded so much that you clearly have far more boxes than you need, feel free to dispose of the extras immediately.

# Store by material

To be frank, the way I decide where to store things is quite approximate, but the end result still looks unified because I consider materials. When planning the overall layout of storage spaces, I keep in mind the material that each thing is made of, such as cloth, paper, or earth and place items made of similar material near each other.

**My three main material categories are cloth, paper and electric**, simply because these are the easiest to identify, the most numerous, and often the most scattered around the house. Things that fall under 'cloth', such as aprons, cloth bags, and sheets, I store near clothes, which are representative of this category. Things like documents, notebooks, memo pads, postcards and envelopes I store near bookshelves because books are the king of the 'paper' category. The 'electric' category consists of electrical appliances, cords, memory sticks and so on. Things such as creams and lotions are classified as 'liquids', food falls under 'foodstuffs', and dishes can be further subdivided into 'ceramics' and 'glass'.

Of course, you can't store everything on the basis of material categories alone. For one thing, not every item can be easily classified as a single material, and things within the same category may be made of different materials. The point is just to keep materials in mind when storing. This makes the end result much neater and keeps storage simple.

I developed this approach after trying a broad range of methods, and I find that it produces a completely different level of neatness once everything is stored. Each material generates its own unique aura. Cloth and paper items, which are made of plant materials, for example, breathe and seem to radiate warmth. Plastic, on the other hand, is much denser. It doesn't breathe at all and makes the chest feel tighter. Televisions, electric cords and other items have a slightly pungent electrical smell. Placing items with similar vibes close together seems to intensify the impression of neatness, perhaps because their auras are compatible. This is one point on which all my clients who have tried storing things by material agree.

Houses in which the walls and storage spaces are all made of wood have a very different feel from those with predominantly metal furnishings. The same is true for rooms with many books compared to those with a lot of electrical items. Materials determine the feeling of a space, which is why it is so important to consider them when planning your storage. As a child, I used to enjoy pushing the little globules of oil floating in my ramen bowl into one big blob after all the noodles were gone. The sense of rightness that comes when like materials are stored in one place is similar to the satisfaction I felt when that oily 'continent' formed in the sea of ramen.

# Pack drawers like a Japanese bento box

'I've reduced a lot, but it hasn't clicked yet. I guess I should reduce more, right?' This question was posed to me by K on my third visit to her house. She had already progressed a long way in the tidying process but felt it wasn't finished.

During the tidying process, there comes a moment when you realize that you have just the right amount of stuff. I call this the click point. **It's the moment when, after discarding everything but the things you love, you know that you have all you need to feel content.** Since publishing my first book, I have received quite a few messages from people announcing excitedly that they've found their click point.

In cases like K's, the cause is usually obvious when I examine the contents of the storage spaces. I'll open a drawer and see the clothes inside properly folded and arranged on edge, but there will be space for at least five more outfits. The next drawer will be only half full. In fact, all the storage spaces will seem rather empty. 'I've reduced so much,' my client will explain, 'that I thought I should leave room in case I buy more.' I know how they feel, but this is a booby trap. **The rule of thumb for storage is 90 per cent.** Once you've chosen the things you love, the correct approach is to fill your drawers to the point where they look full but not stuffed.

It's human nature to want to fill in the gaps. If we aim for just 70 per cent full or for 'spacious', not only will we miss our click point but, before we know it, we'll begin to accumulate things that don't bring us joy, end up buying new storage items, and eventually find ourselves back where we started. If you haven't reached the click point, the best approach is to try filling up the spaces in your drawers and cupboards with just the right amount. Often, this alone can instantly result in the discovery that you have enough.

It worked for K. She rearranged her clothes so that drawers were full and then filled any remaining space with writing implements and supplies for bead craft. Before she knew it, the two plastic drawers she had kept on the floor of her room were empty, and everything fit neatly into the main wardrobe.

When storing, think about a Japanese bento box. This boxed lunch is a traditional part of Japanese cuisine, and I think no other culture in the world takes this meal as seriously as Japan does. Presentation is very important and colourful foods are exquisitely arranged in little compartments. Countless recipes are produced every year specifically for bento lunches, and an annual nation-wide contest is held to determine the best train bento.

The bento encapsulates Japan's unique storage space aesthetics. Key concepts include separating flavours, beauty of presentation, and close fit. If you substitute 'separating flavours' for 'separating materials', packing things into a drawer operates on exactly the same principles as packing a bento box.

One other mistake people commonly make when storing things in drawers is using too many dividers. It is fine to separate cotton clothes from wool clothes in a drawer, for example, but there is no need to do so by inserting an inner box or divider. The aim when putting away cloth items is to achieve a comfortably close fit. As clothes are made of plant fibres, they need a certain amount of space to breathe, but not so much that they lose their warmth. Pack them in the drawer with the image of them holding hands or being placed cheek to cheek, and you will feel a great sense of relief.

When storing socks and underwear, it's dangerous to use specialized storage goods that have individual spaces for each item, like silkworm compartments. If you have more than enough storage room, this may not be an issue, but compartmentalized goods are inefficient because they leave excess gaps. Worse still, if there is too much space between your clothes, they will feel chilled and uncomfortable. Squishing them together so tightly that they can't breathe should also be avoided.

The exception is thin and flimsy synthetic fabrics, like polyester, which tend to stretch if they are folded too tightly. These should be packed in a smaller box first to separate them from other materials. In some cases, other types of *komono* that are not made of cloth, such as belts, may also look better when stored with dividers. As long as you can see at a glance what is in the drawer, you're doing fine. Being able to remove things from the drawer easily is just an added bonus, not a necessity.

# The four principles of storage

Gathering everything from one category together is the most 'festive' part of the tidying festival. It starts with clothes. When my clients dump all their clothes in a huge mound on the floor and begin checking which ones spark joy, their excitement rises noticeably. 'This is great! I'm getting the hang of what my joy criterion is!' But by the time we're ready to start storing, we've usually run out of time. 'Oh, I have to go and pick up my kids.'

I would love to keep going, as they're still in the middle of the festivities, but instead I leave them with some homework. I tell them to work on storing until our next lesson and make sure they know **the four principles: fold it, stand it upright, store in one spot, and divide your storage space into square compartments.** These principles apply not only to storing clothes but to every other category as well.

Anything soft and pliable should be folded. This includes not only clothing but also gloves, cloth *komono* items, plastic bags and laundry nets. If it feels soft and pliable, it contains air. Folding helps to deflate it. This reduces its volume and maximizes the amount you can store.

Everything that can be stood on edge on its own without falling over should be stored upright in a drawer, rather than flat, including folded clothes, stationery supplies, medicines and packets of pocket tissues. This not only allows you to take full advantage of the height of your storage space but also is the best way to tell at a glance what is stored where.

Store items from the same category in one spot. If you are living with a family, sort by person first, then by category and finally by type of material. If you follow this order, storage will be much simpler.

The last principle is dividing your storage space into square compartments. Homes are basically a combination of square spaces, and therefore square storage spaces and square compartments within those spaces work best. If you use empty boxes for storing, it's better to choose square boxes rather than round ones.

If the job of selecting what to keep is too overwhelming for you to remember all four principles, just focus on the first two. *'If it's folded, it'll be fine! If it stands upright, it'll be fine!'* Use this as your storing mantra, and you're sure to find that you need far less space and that the inside of your drawer is neat and tidy in no time.

# Fold clothes like origami

E was working on her clothes. She had just finished the 'joy check' and, after a lesson on the basics, had begun folding. As a general rule, my clients fold their own clothes, but I do help if there is a huge amount. Silently we got to work, sitting side by side on the floor of her room, which was piled high with the clothes she wished to keep and bags filled with those she had bid farewell.

I folded a hooded parka, a T-shirt with gathers and a large ribbon on the front, a crossover top of jersey material with frilly sleeves, a dolman-sleeved knit top that reminded me of a flying squirrel, a cardigan with elongated triangular sleeves . . . This went on for about ten minutes until I realized something was odd. She seemed to have so many unusually shaped clothes. I continued to fold but this time kept an eye on what E was doing. She folded a simple T-shirt followed by a tube top, but when she picked up an asymmetrical knit bolero jacket, she slipped it into my pile. So that's what was going on! All the strangely shaped and hard-to-fold clothes were ending up in my pile.

'Now just a minute, E!' I exclaimed.

'I'm sorry,' she said. 'I couldn't help myself. I could never fold something like that.'

Modern fashions increasingly feature irregularly

shaped hems and sleeves. When faced with the wide-necked, odd-shaped cardigans that are currently in vogue, you might wonder how on earth to even start folding them, while sleeves as limp as seaweed will make you want to throw in the towel. But the secret to folding odd-shaped clothes is this: never give up. Clothes are simply rectangular pieces of cloth sewn together. Regardless of how it looks, any garment can always be folded into a rectangle. If you come across an odd-shaped one, take a deep breath and remain calm. Spread it out on the floor or other large, flat surface so that you can see the shape of the cloth. This will show you where extra cloth has been added for volume and how the garment was put together. From this perspective, the shape makes much more sense and is no longer daunting.

Once you've grasped the shape, then follow the basic rules, folding both arms over towards the centre of the garment to form a rectangle. If the sleeves are particularly wide, fold them several times to prevent them from protruding from the rectangle's edge. Once you have folded it into a long rectangle with the body of the outfit as the centre, fold it in half and then fold it again one or two more times.

**Folding works best if you approach it like origami.** After each fold, smooth your hand over the whole garment in a soothing motion, before going on to the next fold. While you don't need to make a sharp crease by running your fingernail along the edge as you would in origami, if you apply a firm pressure, the garment will keep its shape long term. Sound like so much work you might give up halfway? Don't worry. Just try it once. Having folded your clothes carefully and properly once, the next time will be that much easier, as if your clothes remember that shape. After a month of folding like this, you will no longer need a flat surface but will be able to fold your clothes on your knees or in the air. After all, most Japanese people can fold paper cranes as if there were nothing to it.

Using the palm of your hand is the key. If you've been folding with just your fingertips, try applying your palm, which emanates a sort of warm 'hand power'. That warmth causes the fibres on the garment to stand up and pulls the cloth taut, like paper, making it easy to fold your clothes like origami. If you smooth the cloth with the palm of your hand and fold the garment like origami until it becomes smaller than you might expect, your folded clothes will stand on their own and can be stored upright.

Children's clothes, by the way, should not be folded like adult clothes, because they make such thick little bundles that they won't stay folded. Instead, reduce the number of folds until you find the rectangular shape that they can hold best.

# Everything you need to know about the KonMari folding method

If you can make a rectangle by folding the edges towards the centre of the garment, you have mastered about 90 per cent of the KonMari folding method. No matter the garment, this is the goal. Folding a garment often reminds me of the priests who carve Buddhist statues. They gaze intently at a piece of wood until they see the shape of the figure within it and carve the wood until it emerges. While I know it's a whole different dimension, the idea is similar. Spread out the piece of clothing, gaze at it intently, and, once you find the rectangular shape within it, take the pieces on the outside of that rectangle and fold them inside it.

## BASIC FOLDING METHOD

1. Fold both edges of the body of the garment towards the centre to form a rectangle.

2. Fold the rectangle in half lengthwise.

3. Fold this in half or in thirds.

The first rectangle is quite long. Folding it in half helps to reinforce the garment's shape. When folding, grasp the thinner or weaker part of the garment, which is the neck for tops and the legs for trousers. Rather than

# Basic folding method

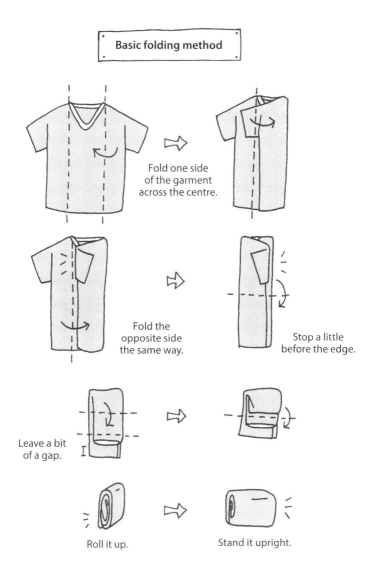

Fold one side of the garment across the centre.

Fold the opposite side the same way.

Stop a little before the edge.

Leave a bit of a gap.

Roll it up.

Stand it upright.

folding it all the way to the edge of the bottom layer, leave a little gap. The goal of these two steps is to create a firmer, cleaner shape, so please adjust the part you grasp and the width of the gap to suit the garment. After that, all you need to do is adjust for height by folding again either in half or in thirds for most clothes. For extra-long clothes, you may need to fold four or five times. There are many little tricks to folding, but basically you have done it right if the end result is a smooth rectangle.

These rectangles will be stored standing upright in your drawers, but before you store them, check whether they can stand independently by placing each one upright on the floor. If it doesn't fall over when you remove your hand, it has passed the test and won't collapse when placed in your drawer, even when you take out or put back other items. If, however, it collapses weakly, the folds need readjusting. Perhaps the rectangle is too wide or the height of the folds in step 2 or 3 is too high or too low, making the rectangle too thick. For some garments, it may work better to skip step 2 and go directly to folding it in thirds. As you experiment, you will find the way that works just perfectly for that particular garment – what I call the 'golden point of folding'.

Of course, there are always exceptions. For example, the first step for some types of garments could be to fold the garment in half lengthwise. The reason my basic method calls for folding the edges towards the centre first to make a rectangle is to avoid creasing the centre of the garment. Creases in the centre make clothes look wrinkled. Garments that look fine with a crease down the centre, however, can be folded in half lengthwise. These include ribbed or wrinkle-processed fabrics, which don't show wrinkles anyway, and cardigans or other clothes that are already designed with a line down the middle. Wrinkles don't usually matter for sportswear either.

There are some clothes that even when folded properly will not stand upright. Materials that are thin and flimsy, such as polyester, or soft and bulky, such as fleece and long-gauge knits, will not hold their shape when folded. Rather than trying to force them to stand up, lay them flat after you've folded them. For folding instructions for specific items, see chapter 4.

# Plan storage with the idea of getting rid of furniture used for storing

Although the finer details will depend on the design of your house, there are two iron rules for deciding where to store things: **use built-in storage units first and store large things first.**

We'll start by looking at how to use built-in storage units. First, however, remember the ideal lifestyle that you imagined when you began your tidying marathon. If you have photos or clippings, take a good long look at those. I'm sure that many of you will realize that your ideal was more spacious and neater than what you see in your house at this point. Then how can you make your home more spacious? The answer is simple: get rid of furniture. But by furniture, I don't mean your bed or your sofa; I mean furniture that is used to store things.

I can just hear people saying, 'Impossible!' But I assure you, it is, in fact, totally possible. When I give lessons, I have no intention of using any other storage but that which already comes with the house. No matter what the current state of a house is, when I imagine what it will look like after tidying is complete, I envision each room exactly the way it was when it was first made. I imagine how it will appear after all the clear plastic boxes and bookcases occupying the floor have been put away in the closets and cupboards and it seems brand new. My clients find it hard to believe when I assure them that this is how their home will look, but I am almost always right. There are times when a client has more things that bring him or her joy in the end, making the result slightly different from what I had imagined. However, as long as I proceed with the image of the house on the day it was born, the final product achieves a much higher standard.

The key to success in storage is to start by filling the built-in storage spaces on the assumption that they can accommodate everything you own. In addition to wardrobes and cupboards, I also consider any units attached to furniture as built-in storage, such as drawers under the bed or shelves on the TV stand. Also included are any pieces of furniture you have no intention of discarding, such as dressing tables or heirloom wardrobes. If your home has no built-in storage spaces, it's fine to use whatever furniture you have, in the order of those that give you the most joy first.

As for the second rule, storing large items first, by 'large' I simply mean things with a large volume, such as clear plastic drawers storing your folded clothes, seasonal items such as space heaters and fans and clothes racks. Put these items away in the built-in storage spaces first. If you decide later that any of them belong in the room rather than in the wardrobe, you can take them out. But putting the large items away in the wardrobes and cupboards first, and then fitting the smaller items into the leftover spaces, powerfully stimulates the 'storage brain', resulting in storage that seems to fit just right. People are often surprised to hear that it's easier to store things when space is limited, but I believe restrictions force our brains to think at full capacity, which helps us create better storage.

# Ideal storage weaves a rainbow in your home

In this book, we look at how to store items that are common to most homes but that can present difficulties when deciding where to store them. For *komono* items not mentioned, as long as you follow the first and foremost rule of storing by category, you should be fine. Feel free to make up your own categories for things that don't fall into such standards as stationery supplies, electrical cords, medicines and tools. For example, people who enjoy art might want an 'art supplies' category. If you are like one of my clients who loved collecting labels so much she had two drawers full of them, you can make an independent 'label' category. For someone with many interests and all the equipment to go with them, from calligraphy to sewing, it may help to make a general 'hobby equipment' category. A standard solution for surplus laundry detergent and sponges that won't fit in one place is to designate a separate category for 'consumable supplies' and dedicate an entire drawer to them in a cupboard or storage room.

Remember to store things of similar nature near each other. Storing should go very smoothly if you repeat this step each time. Some people store their digital camera next to computer items because they have the same electric feel, while to others, the logical neighbour for their computer is stationery supplies because for them, both categories fall under the larger category of 'things for daily use'. The process is really like a word association game. As you go along, you'll soon find that similar things naturally end up side by side. In reality, seemingly separate categories overlap each other slightly, existing in a gradation of interconnection. By intuiting and searching for those connections and storing like things near each other, the gradation will become more obvious. In that sense, storing your possessions is like weaving a beautiful rainbow in your home. And, because it is a gradation, you do not need to worry if the boundaries between categories are a little blurred.

In the end, you've succeeded if you know where everything in your house belongs and if the layout feels natural to both you and your things. **If your intuition tells you that this might be the place, then, for now at least, it is most certainly right.** When considering what category something falls into and where it should be stored, it's important not to think too deeply or carefully. As long as you have chosen the things that you love, then relax and enjoy the rest of the process.

I can say with confidence that there's no task more enjoyable than storing. You're creating a home for the things you love while exploring their interconnections. While this may not seem to be concrete, this intuitive approach to storage is the best and most natural way to make your house comfortable for you. Tidying is the task of bringing your home closer to its natural state. So it's a natural part of yourself.

PART II

The tidying encyclopaedia

# 4
# Tidying clothes

Your tidying campaign starts with clothes. Gather every item of clothing you own from every corner of your house and pile them all in one spot. Do it swiftly and mechanically, like a robot. When you think you are done, take one last look and ask yourself, 'Is this really everything?' Did you perhaps forget something that got into someone else's drawer? Be committed enough to discard anything that you've overlooked, except those things that are currently in the laundry.

# Tops

Once you have your mountain of clothes, it's time for the 'joy check.' Hold each item in your hands and choose the ones that spark joy. As I discussed in chapter 1, start with tops because things worn closer to your heart make it easier to judge whether or not you feel joy. You can also define things that spark joy as things that make you happy. If you love an outfit because it keeps you warm, for example, you can keep it with confidence.

If you don't think it's something you'll want to see again, then thank it for all it has done and say goodbye. Bag the clothes that don't spark joy and give them to charity or take them to a used-clothing shop.

## How to fold shirts

To see how to fold short-sleeved tops, refer to the basic folding method instructions on page 71.

For long-sleeved tops, once you've decided the width you want the folded garment to be, follow the basic procedure of folding the edges towards the centre to make a rectangle. The trick is to bring the sleeve all the way over to the opposite edge, and then to fold the sleeve down towards the bottom, following the line of the garment. The aim is to avoid having the sleeves overlapping each other, which would add bulk.

## How to fold long-sleeved tops

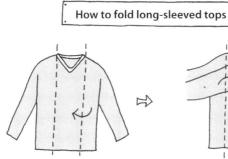

Fold one side
towards the centre.

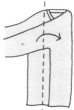

Fold the sleeve
to fit within the
rectangle's width.

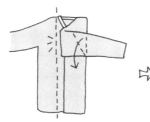

Fold the sleeve back
flush with the edge
of the rectangle.

Fold the other side
the same way.

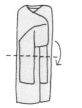

Fold almost but not
quite to the edge.

Fold in thirds to fit the
height of the storage
space.

Stand it up.

In my first book, I said that how you fold sleeves is up to you, and this is also what I taught my clients in my private lessons. For many years, I thought the way I folded long sleeves was quite common, and therefore I did not see the need to explain it in detail. When I demonstrated this method to a magazine reporter, however, she said, 'That's quite a unique way of folding, isn't it?' For the first time, I realized that most people fold sleeves sideways in two or three layers. The way I do it may not seem that different, but I urge you to try it. When you run your hand over the final product, you'll see that there is almost no perceptible lump where the sleeve is, and the garment stays folded without collapsing.

For garments with dolman sleeves, fold the sleeves in the same way that you would normally fold a garment, and in no time, you will have a rectangle. If it has a frilly hem, fold the garment in half so that the hem is on the inside.

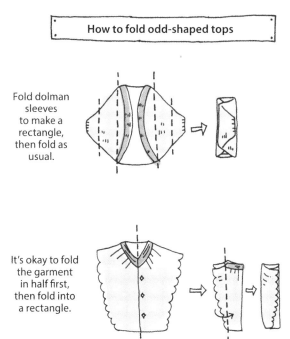

Fold dolman
sleeves
to make a
rectangle,
then fold as
usual.

It's okay to fold
the garment
in half first,
then fold into
a rectangle.

Once you have made a
rectangle, fold the usual way
to the right height.

## How to fold camisoles

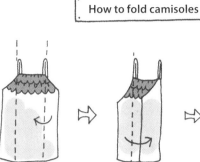

Fold one side
towards the centre.

Fold the
other side the
same way.

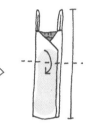

Fold in half,
including the straps.

Don't forget to
leave a space.

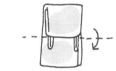

Make a smooth
rectangle.

## How to fold camisoles

The straps on camisoles are neither extensions nor decorations. Without them, the camisole can't do its job, so treat them as an integral part of it. This means that after you have folded in the sides so that the camisole is one-third its original width, the whole thing, including the straps, should be folded in half. From there on, you can follow the regular folding procedure to adjust the final bundle to the height you want. Ribbed or very thin fabric makes it difficult to fold a camisole in thirds across the bodice. In such cases, it works better to fold it in half.

Camisoles made of polyester and other flimsy fabric will not stand upright when folded the regular way. Begin as usual by folding the sides across the centre and then folding in half lengthwise. At that point, roll the garment up from the fold and it will stay rolled more easily. In many cases, it still won't stand up on its own, but rather than criticizing it for this failure, recognize that its charm is the fact that it is so small it can slip easily into any little space in your storage unit. The other clothes will hold it up. This trick will also work for other floppy clothes, such as chiffon blouses.

## How to fold parkas and polo necks

As usual, fold both sides towards the centre of the garment to make a rectangle. Then fold the protruding hood or turtleneck, which is essentially extraneous, into the rectangle. This simplifies the shape, and from there you just need to fold the garment to fit your storage unit. If the neck does not extend very far, then folding it inside the rectangle will make it bulkier. In such cases, just fold it the normal way, without folding in the neck.

## How to fold thick tops

If you try to fold thick, bulky garments like long-gauge jumpers and fleece into compact bundles so that they will stand, they will only expand with air anyway, so fold them relatively loosely. If they won't stand up in your drawer, it's all right to lay them down. They do, however, take up a lot of room even when folded properly, and therefore, during the off-season, it's better to store them more compactly.

Half of the volume is air, so the best solution is to use a tight-fitting bag, such as a cloth shopping bag or drawstring bag. Press down on the garment to deflate it as you insert it into the bag. Any bag will do as long as it is made of woven rather than non-woven fabric, or you could

# How to fold parkas

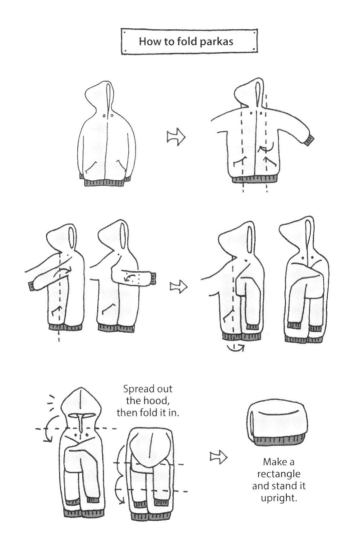

Spread out the hood, then fold it in.

Make a rectangle and stand it upright.

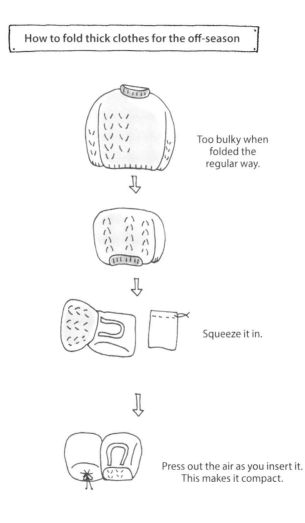

Too bulky when folded the regular way.

Squeeze it in.

Press out the air as you insert it. This makes it compact.

even use a *furoshiki* (traditional square Japanese wrapping cloth) or a large scarf. The key is to use something that is about two sizes too small so that it deflates the garment like a vacuum bag.

## How to fold tops with decorations

Decorations are delicate. They come off easily, snag on other clothes, and can be damaged while taking them out or putting them in the drawer. Therefore, they need to be handled with extra loving care. When I look at tops with multiple decorations, I first consider which part requires the most protection. The garment should be folded so that this part is on the inside. If the decorations are on the bodice, fold the garment so that the part without decorations is on the outside. If it has frills, lace, or other ornamentation on the bottom hem, pick up the hem rather than the neck when you fold it in half after folding in the arms. If you cannot see the decorations once it is folded, you have done it correctly. The buttons on cardigans and the collars on polo shirts should also be folded inside the garment in order to protect them.

# Bottoms

Sort bottoms by category, such as trousers, jeans, skirts, and so on. If you find that you have a lot of one thing, such as white skirts or jeans, and aren't sure which to keep, try them on and think objectively about how often you wear them. If you have not worn something for years, you will almost certainly never wear it again. Bottoms support your lower body, so choose ones that spark joy.

The rule for storage is to fold trousers that are made of cotton, such as jeans, but to hang those that are more formal, such as suit trousers and ones with a centre crease. When hanging skirts, you can save space by hanging two skirts from the same hanger, preferably two that are similar colours or shapes.

## How to fold trousers and shorts

Fold one trouser leg on top of the other. Fold the legs up towards the waistband but not quite touching it, and then fold this in thirds again. This is the basic method for folding trousers, but please adjust the number of times you fold the legs to suit the length. Shorts only need to be folded once lengthwise and then once in half. Although it may seem like a bit of a curve ball, shorts that have more volume, such as wide-legged culottes and woollen shorts, often work best if you begin by folding them in thirds. After that, fold them in half.

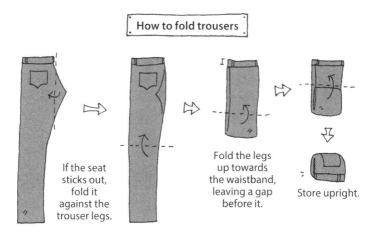

## How to fold trousers

If the seat sticks out, fold it against the trouser legs.

Fold the legs up towards the waistband, leaving a gap before it.

Store upright.

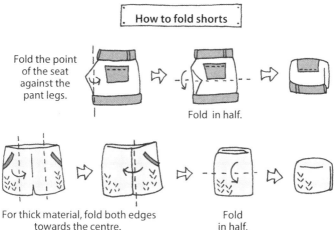

## How to fold shorts

Fold the point of the seat against the pant legs.

Fold in half.

For thick material, fold both edges towards the centre.

Fold in half.

If the seat of a pair of trousers sticks out after you've folded it in half, you can make a neater rectangle by folding the protruding piece back against the trousers. A clerk in a boutique taught me this trick, and it was an eye-opener for me as I do not own a single pair of long trousers.

## Dresses and skirts

One of my clients, a self-professed 'dress fanatic' and successful businesswoman who has a whole wardrobe of them, calls the dress her 'combat uniform'. Dresses should be hung to take full advantage of their visual capacity to spark joy, but if you need to fold them, please use the illustration as a guide. If you are wondering whether to hang or fold a skirt, the rule of thumb is to hang only those items that look happier when hung. Fluttery skirts should therefore generally be hung, but it is still convenient to know how to fold them for times when you are travelling or if you do not have enough hanger space.

## How to fold dresses

No matter how wide the skirt, fold it so it forms a rectangle.

Fold the edge not quite to the other side, then fold in half lengthwise.

Fold or roll it to fit the height of your storage unit.

## How to fold skirts

Fold into a rectangle.

Fold almost in half, leaving a space between the belt and hem, then fold again two or three times or roll it to fit the height of the space.

Your skirt becomes a rectangle, too.

95

## How to fold garments with wide hems

I can certainly understand if you are daunted by the thought of folding a skirt or dress with a hem as wide as the bottom of Mount Fuji. But no matter how wide it seems, don't be afraid. Spread it out calmly and you will see that, like all types of clothing, it is simply a combination of two triangles and a rectangle. All you need to do is fold the triangular pieces on either side inside the rectangle.

If it's excessively wide, you can adjust by folding the triangular pieces more times. If the cloth is too thin and flimsy to control, start by folding the garment in half lengthwise first. As long as it becomes a rectangle, you can then follow the basic order of folding it in half and then folding it several times more, or rolling it until it is the desired height.

# Clothes that hang

Clothes made of thicker materials, such as jackets, suits, and coats, should be stored on hangers, as should any items that are hard to fold or that wrinkle easily, such as men's dress shirts and garments that are made of fluttery material.

Some of the items hanging in your wardrobe may have been very expensive, which could make you reluctant to get rid of them. This, however, is precisely the time to apply the joy check even more seriously. If it doesn't spark joy when you hold it, yet you can't bring yourself to discard it, try it on. Stand in front of the mirror and ask yourself, 'Do I want to wear this out somewhere?' Think about it dispassionately.

When hanging clothes, be sure to arrange them so that they rise to the right. Keep the same category of clothes together: coats with coats, suits with suits, jackets with jackets, and so on.

# Socks and stockings

Gather not only socks and stockings that are currently in use, but also any extras that are still in their packages. If you have a lot, sort them by category: socks, stockings, tights, and leggings. Some people think it doesn't really matter if they wear socks with holes in them or tights that are pilled, but this is like declaring 'today doesn't really matter'. Your feet bear your weight and help you live your life, and it is your socks that cradle those feet. The socks you wear at home are particularly important because they are the contact point between you and your house, so choose ones that will make the time you spend there even more enjoyable.

Balling your socks and stockings, or tying them into knots, is cruel. Please put an end to this practice today.

## How to fold socks

Lay one sock against the other and fold as many times as needed depending on the length of the socks. This is the simplest item, which makes it a great place to start if you want to teach your children how to fold.

## How to fold stockings

First, fold one leg over the other, then grasp the toes and fold the stockings in thirds. Finally, roll them up like a

## How to fold stockings, socks, and thick tights

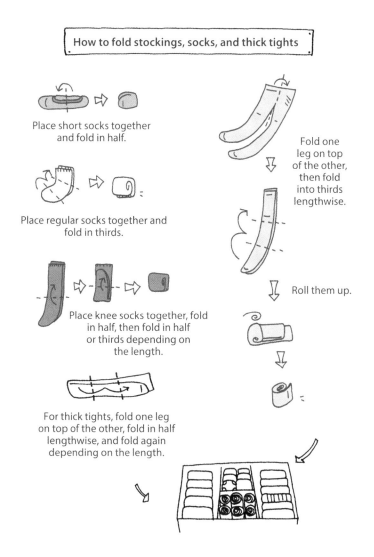

Place short socks together and fold in half.

Place regular socks together and fold in thirds.

Place knee socks together, fold in half, then fold in half or thirds depending on the length.

For thick tights, fold one leg on top of the other, fold in half lengthwise, and fold again depending on the length.

Fold one leg on top of the other, then fold into thirds lengthwise.

Roll them up.

sushi roll and stand them on edge. As stockings unravel easily, it works best to stand them up in a box with dividers first and then put the box in the drawer.

## How to fold thick tights

Although tights are the same shape as stockings, if they are quite thick, fold them like trousers rather than rolling them like stockings. Stockings are only rolled because the material is too thin to fold properly. If you are rolling tights and find that they are too thick or too stiff, it's a sign that they would prefer to be folded.

# Underwear

The underwear category includes not only knickers and bras but also such items as long winter underwear and slips. Underwear is by far the top item my clients want to replace when they finish tidying up. Undergarments may be invisible from the outside, but you should turn your 'joy sensor' on full when choosing which to keep because they are in direct contact with your body. Even those that are plain and practical, if they make you happy because they keep you warm or make you feel comfortable, belong with those clothes that spark joy.

## How to fold underwear

When folding knickers, which are often made of light and flimsy material, you will have better success if you focus on making them quite small. The crotch is the most delicate part and should be folded inside, while decorations such as a bow on the centre of the waistband should be folded to show on the outside. Begin by spreading out a pair with the back facing upward. Fold the crotch up to just under the waistband. Fold the sides over so that the crotch is wrapped inside, then roll up from the bottom. When you turn the knickers over, they should be shaped like a spring roll with only the front of the waistband showing.

Undergarments that are too smooth and silky to stay folded, such as slips, can be folded and rolled. If your underwear is made of thin material that unrolls as soon as you finish folding it, it's best to store them in a smaller box. A tissue box works well because it's the same width as knickers. One tissue box can store about seven pairs. Of course, another type of box will also do as long as it fits your knickers and brings you joy. Those that are more like strings than underwear tend to collapse when folded, and it's therefore best to store them in your small box or fit them in with other clothes that will hold them up.

Rolling underwear made of cotton or other thick fabric will only make them thicker so that they take up more space. Instead of rolling in the last step, it's better to fold them.

## How to fold knickers

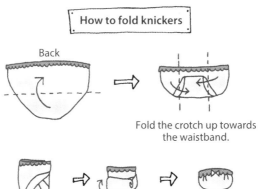

Back

Fold the crotch up towards the waistband.

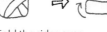

Fold the sides over the crotch and roll.

Turn over to show the pretty decoration on the waistband.

## How to fold boxers and briefs

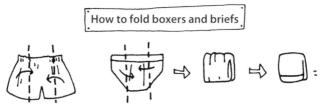

Fold the edges across the middle to make a rectangle; fold in half and then in thirds.

For boxers and briefs, fold the edges across the middle to make a rectangle, then fold in half and then in thirds. Any other undergarments should be folded and stored like regular clothes.

## Light colours in front, dark colours behind

Store your underwear with lighter colours at the front of the drawer and move towards darker colours in the back. When you line your underwear up like this, your drawer will look like a box of sweets. Clients frequently report that their underwear drawer looks so beautiful that they can't resist opening it to gaze at the contents. The same principles apply to men's boxers and briefs. Arrange them from light to dark.

Clients often ask what they should do if they have more than one row of underwear, or whether it's okay to put leftover underwear in spaces between other clothes. The answer is yes, as long as when you open the drawer, you can see at a glance that the gradation moves from light colours in front to dark colours in the back. There is no hard-and-fast rule, so try experimenting to see what storage method brings you joy. Because that, of course, is what really matters – your own sense of joy. See what works for you as if you were carrying on a dialogue with your things and your home. The inspiration you get from that conversation is bound to be the right method for you. **Now that you've learned how to select the**

**things that bring you joy, believe in your intuition.** The joy factor never lies.

Living in a clean and tidy space automatically improves your self-image, and you'll find it hard to stand any discrepancy between your surroundings, which bring you so much joy, and the undergarments you are wearing. That's part of the wonderful magic of tidying up.

## Store bras like royalty

Brassieres rank highest on the list of things that my clients replace as soon as they finish tidying up. Of all the messages I receive after my lessons, the most unusual are the ones I call 'bra declarations': statements such as 'My worn-out bras have finally left home,' 'My bras, which were long past their best-before date, have gone travelling,' and 'Senior members of my bra collection have retired.'

I doubt whether there is any other profession that affords such an intimate examination of other people's underwear. From this perspective, I would have to say that the way people treat their undergarments reveals much about their personality.

First, knickers and bras should be stored separately. I sometimes come across people who press a pair of knickers into their bra cups to make a set. While there is nothing wrong with this, I do encourage you to try treating your bras like royalty just once. Compared to other clothes, they have exceptional pride and emit a distinctive aura. Bras are never seen when worn, despite their uncommon shape and varied designs with decorative frills and lace. They are more like an invisible accessory than clothing and should therefore be stored so as to retain their shape and respect their beauty.

A common and unfortunate mistake is to flatten the cups and then line them up. This is a waste. Instead, arrange bras so that they rest lightly in layers against one another. If you fold the shoulder straps and side pieces inside the cups, you can reinforce the cups and easily extract a bra without disturbing the rest of the row.

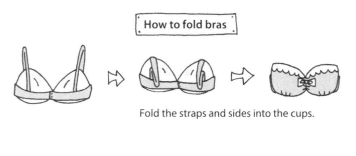

**How to fold bras**

Fold the straps and sides into the cups.

Arranging them in a colour gradation will increase your joy when looking at them. When my clients switch to this method, their faces always light up. 'It's just like a store display!' they exclaim. Interestingly, all of my clients report that when they treat their bras with more respect, they also become more respectful towards other things.

What would be the ideal home for a bra? In my book, the ultimate approach would be to dedicate an entire wooden or rattan drawer to them. Whatever you decide to do, please make an exclusive home for your bras. That alone can fill your heart with joy.

Tidying up your bras is actually a great way to enhance the joy factor. My clients are usually eager to shop for new bras as soon as they've finished tidying them. On average, they will have purchased new ones within a week, and quite a few even leave the house with me to go bra shopping as soon as the lesson is over. Once, one of my clients announced, *'This bra doesn't spark any joy!'* To my surprise, she removed the plain black bra she was wearing right in front of me and placed it in the garbage bag. At our next lesson, this same client, with obvious delight, presented her bra drawer. Displayed in a rattan basket that she had formerly used to store towels, they looked very elegant and colourful.

# A clothes wardrobe that sparks joy

Storing your clothes is easy. First, hang the clothes that you are storing on hangers on the pole. If you have too many to hang, fold as many as possible to save space and store them in a set of drawers placed underneath the pole. Use these drawers to store clothing-related *komono* as well, and any other *komono* categories that seem to fit, such as accessories and items you use daily.

In general, the shelf in the top of the wardrobe is for bags, hats, off-season *komono*, and sentimental items. If more than one person uses the wardrobe, be sure to assign individual space for each person. If you have any clear plastic cases or shelf units, I recommend using these as storage units and placing them inside the wardrobe, too, if there is room. If you have just moved in and don't have any drawers to store your clothes, the perfect time to purchase some is when you've finished your joy check.

If you have a walk-in wardrobe, fully exploit its impressive depth and width. Choose deep drawers that fit the wardrobe perfectly for storing folded clothes. The upper shelf can also be used to store seasonal items and things that are only used occasionally, such as holiday decorations and recreational goods.

The great attraction of walk-in wardrobes is the fact that they are deep. Yet the plain walls can look very broad and bleak. As I mentioned earlier, this gives you a perfect opportunity to add some essence of joy. One of

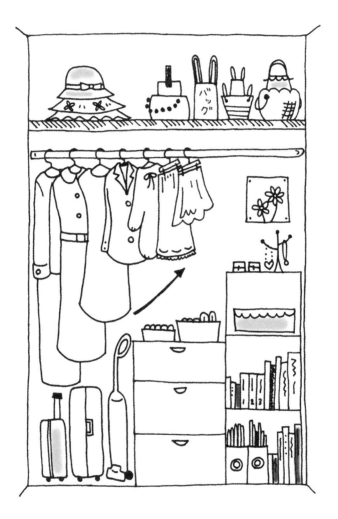

my clients covered a corner of her wardrobe with her wedding pictures and stored all her wedding-related items in this spot, including the welcome board and the ring cushion case. 'I would have felt a bit embarrassed to display these things where everyone could see them. Now, I just have to open my wardrobe door to bring back that same feeling of joy I had on my wedding day.' The shy smile on the face of this normally dry and businesslike client brought back sweet memories for me, too.

The wardrobe is a space where you are free to do whatever you want. One client who really enjoyed coming up with creative solutions used the space below as a parking spot for her children's ride-on toys. The latter proved to be quite popular because the children made a game out of parking their toys when they put them away. **If you view the walk-in wardrobe as a small room, you will be able to create a beautiful storage space.**

My approach to wardrobes evolved from my own experience. I was therefore astounded one day to discover that I wasn't the first. While visiting the Yayoi Museum in Bunkyo Ward, Tokyo, I saw an illustration of the ultimate Japanese closet storage. Entitled 'Closet Ideas', it showed a wardrobe with a bookcase inside it. A beautiful doll rested on top while a pretty cloth had been draped over the shelves to conceal them. The illustration was printed in *Himawari*, a popular girls' magazine published by the famous Junichi Nakahara in 1948. Obviously, over sixty years earlier someone was not only using the Japanese wardrobe in a Western style but was making it beautiful to boot. The illustration embodied my theory that the wardrobe should be considered an extension of the room. It is a marvellous storage space that can be decorated just like a room and concealed behind closed doors.

## To decide where to store something is to give it a home

Many people place their clothes drawers on the bottom of their wardrobes. But what is the best way to organize the contents of those drawers? It's easier to achieve a sense of joy from the contents if we aim for a natural state that feels right.

For example, if a dresser has several drawers, then it is more natural to keep the lightest things at the top and the heaviest at the bottom. Tops would thus be kept in the upper drawers, bottoms, in the lower drawers. Likewise, light materials such as cotton would be kept in the upper drawers and thick, heavy materials, such as wool, in the lower drawers. It is also more natural to put things that we wear on our head or close to it, such as scarves and hats, near the top. If you apply this principle, you'll have an 'uplifting' set of drawers, and that, combined with the principle of hanging clothes so that

they rise to the right, will create an ideal storage space that sparks joy.

Gradate the colours so that you can see at a glance where everything is and also grasp the colour trend of your wardrobe. In general, dark colours should be in the back of the drawer and light colours in the front. Arrange them with the image of a wave of joy surging towards you, and you'll experience a rush of pleasure every time you open the drawer.

Once you've achieved an overall balance, it's time to take a closer look inside each drawer. **Think of your wardrobe as the world of nature and the interior of your drawers as the home in which your things belong.** A sense of stability and order are essential if you are to create a space where your things can relax and get the rest they need. As mentioned earlier, 90 per cent full is best when storing clothes in a drawer, but garments made from thin materials, such as knickers, stockings and slips, need to be packed a little tighter so that they don't unroll.

If your drawers are very deep, you can also store things in layers within the same drawer by filling the bottom of the drawer with folded clothes and then resting a shallow, removable box holding more folded clothes on top.

You can also make the drawer look neat and tidy by keeping the various clothing-related *komono* in a separate box inside it. For example, removable bra straps, ties, and buttons that you just can't throw away can be kept in a ring box.

Some people may think that paying attention to such details makes no difference. It's true that the joy effect of storage is not immediately apparent. Compared to the drama of reducing, where garbage bags pile up each day and your space undergoes a drastic transformation, storage involves quietly moving things around and finding joy in small accomplishments. But there is one thing you need to keep in mind. Tidying up in the true sense of the word does not, by any means, end with reducing alone. You must select a comfortable storage place for each item you have decided to keep, one where each can shine to its full potential. The things you have chosen support your life. You must create a space where they can feel at home.

Personally, I feel that **the essence of the storage process is to appreciate the things you own and to strive to make your relationship with them as special as possible.** To decide where to store something is to give it a home. I can assure you that after you have brought your storage in line with the 'joy specifications', you will experience benefits that you could never have achieved by merely getting rid of things.

## Bag-in-bag method

Store similar bags together.
The bags will support each other.
It's best to store just one bag
inside another.

## How to fold cloth and plastic bags

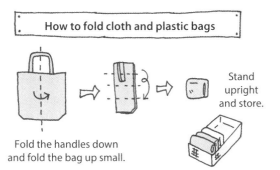

Stand
upright
and store.

Fold the handles down
and fold the bag up small.

# Bags

Bags should be treated as part of the clothing category because they are stored in the wardrobe, too. Are you still hanging on to handbags that you once used every day but have since replaced with similar ones? This seems to be a very common phenomenon among people with a lot of bags. Despite having so many, they usually have very few that they can actually use. If you do not consciously undertake a changing of the guard, the ones you like will become buried within the mountain of those that are never used. At least, that's what happened to me.

Once you've finished choosing your bags, use the 'bag-in-bag' method in which one bag is stored inside another. Foldable bags, such as cloth carrying bags, can be stored folded up.

# Clothing accessories

From belts, hats, gloves and ties to fur collars and pins that have been removed from a coat and stored separately – I refer to all of these as clothing accessories and classify them as clothing *komono*. You may have accessories from clothes that you no longer own or a hood for which you can no longer match a coat. To keep such items 'just in case' you find another use for them is hazardous. Accept the fact that you will never use them again and bid them farewell.

Once you have finished choosing, your storage will look neat in no time if you fold scarves, wool hats, and other foldable items in a dresser drawer, and store non-foldable items in a smallish box inside a drawer or out in the open like a store display.

## Make accessory storage as attractive as possible

In Japan there is a saying that 'beauty is not built in a day'. Even if it takes time, make accessory storage as handsome as possible. When I'm working with a client to make accessory storage from scratch, we spend more time on this per inch of storage space than on any other item. I highly recommend arranging your accessories so that the inside of your drawer looks like a showcase so that every time you open it, it will give you a thrill of joy.

If you don't have a dressing table, you can use a drawer in a chest of drawers or the shallow top drawer in your desk. Mobilize small empty boxes as dividers. In addition to the boxes the accessories came in, including the lids as well as the bottoms, try boxes with separate compartments, such as boxes for chocolate. Although using empty boxes you already have on hand is quick and convenient, you may worry that this could detract from the appearance. They must, of course, pass the test. A tissue box, for example, will not do because it's too ordinary. I recommend sturdy boxes covered in crepe or tissue paper.

If you don't have any boxes like that lying around, don't worry. Once in the drawer, only the bottom is visible. Even plain boxes will work if you put a piece of pretty paper on the bottom. This is your chance to use things that sparked joy but haven't yet been put to use – postcards, wrapping paper, and bags with patterns that you liked can all be cut to fit in the box.

Small dishes also work as accessory containers. One of my clients housed her accessories in a Scandinavian glass ashtray that she loved and had bought on impulse, and the effect was quite beautiful. As an alternative to a drawer, a cosmetic bag or jewellery box can also be used. If you have a jewellery box that you like already, go ahead and use it. Not only are jewellery boxes specifically designed to make accessories look beautiful when placed inside, but they also save time and trouble, representing the easiest way to finish storing your accessories.

If you have a jewellery box, but it doesn't spark joy, you can dismantle it and use the parts. I often startle my clients by grabbing a jewellery box they are about to discard, wrenching off the top with a loud crack and shoving my fingers into either side of the three rows of ring cushions to rip them out. I put the lidless box in the drawer, where it fits snugly, and place the ring cushions in a separate box, transforming these items into the perfect drawer dividers. A playful spirit and a craftsman's temperament make a big difference when making accessory dividers.

Delicate chains and necklaces can be kept untangled by slipping them through slits cut into the edges of the dividers. This is easy to do if you are using boxes made of stiff paper or cardboard. Or you can slightly bend the teeth of a decorative hair comb and string a chain over each tooth.

I also recommend open storage, which means making your accessory storage into a display. If you have a corkboard, use it as an accessory display board. Rather than hanging accessories from ordinary thumb tacks, you can hang them from single pierced earrings for which you have lost the other part of the pair; or you can simply use the earrings as decorations to enliven the display. A simpler method is to use a drawer or box to store the majority of your collection while storing those accessories you wear every day in a small dish or tray out in the open.

## Ties

Ties are accessories for men. Be sure to store them attractively and in such a way that it's easy to choose which one to wear. One way of storing them is to hang them. You can use a necktie hanger, a regular hanger, or, if you have one, the necktie pole on the inside of the wardrobe door.

Another way of storing neckties is to roll them and arrange them in a drawer. You can display them like sushi rolls with the swirly side up, or like a slice of roll cake with the smooth side up.

## Hair accessories

Hair accessories are a common item that people tackle along with regular accessories. If you no longer wear a certain hair tie but love the glittery decorations on it, don't throw it away. Make use of it. Tie it to the neck of a hanger or make it into a curtain tassel. It's fun to make your own original items that spark joy.

As with other accessories, pay attention to appearance when storing them. Storage will look neater if you separate storage compartments by item, such as hair clips or elastic bands, but if you do not have that many items, there is no need to separate them.

## Shoes

People don't generally think of shoes as clothes, but in the KonMari Method they are included in the clothing category and subjected to the joy check early on. Once you have gathered your shoes from every corner of the house, line them up on newspapers spread across the

floor and group them according to type, such as sandals, trainers, boots, and formal shoes. Pick up each pair to see if it sparks joy. If there are any that do not fit properly and hurt your feet, now is the time to get rid of them. Shoes are important. In Japan, we use the expression 'looking at a person's feet' to mean sizing someone up. If you wear shoes that spark joy, they are bound to lead you to a brighter future.

## Storing shoes: Steadily rising joy

There are only two methods for storing shoes: put them straight onto a shoe rack or directly on your wardrobe shelves, or store them in their boxes first and arrange these in the wardrobe. If you have enough shelves, it's better to line them up without their boxes because the boxes take up unnecessary space. However, if you can fit more than one pair of shoes in each box, this can also be an effective way of storing. Choose shoes that don't lose their shape easily and store them on their sides. Aim to fit two pairs of thin footwear, such as beach sandals, in one box.

A basic principle of storage is to reduce bulk and utilize height. We can't reduce the bulk of shoes, however, and therefore our only choice is to utilize the height of the storage space. Storage goods come in handy for this. Z-shaped inserts take advantage of the height of your shelves by stacking one shoe on top of the other, which doubles the amount of storage space available.

My motto for shoe storage is 'steadily rising joy'. The heaviest things go on the bottom and rise to lighter things on top. Start by designating a space for each person in the house. If you have several shelves per person, put regular shoes, such as pumps and leather shoes, on the bottom and lighter shoes like sandals above them.

## Tips for packing a suitcase

Packing a suitcase for business or leisure trips follows the same basic principles as those for storage in the home. Clothes should be folded and packed upright. Fold suits and lay them flat on top. Pack bras on top, and don't flatten them. Pack small things such as underwear in a travel pouch, and transfer lotions and toiletries into smaller bottles to reduce volume.

I enjoy unpacking even more than packing. As soon as I get home, I remove everything from my suitcase, put the laundry in the washing machine, and return everything else to its proper place. Then I wipe the outside of the suitcase and the wheels. I give myself a time limit of thirty minutes. The key is to pretend you're an unpacking robot and move quickly and efficiently.

**WHAT TO DO ABOUT YOUR FAMILY'S CLOTHES**

One of the questions people who live with their families frequently ask me is, 'When should I tidy up my family's clothes?'

The basic rule of tidying is that you should focus on tidying up your own things first. Once you have finished this task completely, however, you can assist your children or your spouse to tidy their clothes. But be sure to leave the work of choosing what to keep up to them. **From my experience in teaching how to tidy, most children who are three or older can choose what brings them joy.**

If you have family members who are reluctant to discard, just teaching them how to fold the clothes and switching to storing clothes upright will make their space look neater and can often motivate them to start discarding. Even if they have no inclination to tidy up themselves, don't do what I once did and start throwing their things away without asking.

# 5

# Tidying books

## Advice for those who think they can't part with books

I f you believe that books are the one thing you cannot possibly do away with and have been avoiding tidying up for this very reason, that's a terrible waste. Tidying up your books is the best way to increase your sensitivity to joy and your ability to take action.

The most common reason people can't bring themselves to discard a book is because they might want to read it again. But if a book doesn't spark joy for you now, it's almost guaranteed that you'll never read it again some other day. We read books because we seek the experience of reading. Once read, a book has already been 'experienced'. Even if you don't remember the content completely, you have already internalized it.

As for books you've only read halfway, or ones you haven't yet read at all, get rid of the whole lot. Precious books that belong in your personal Hall of Fame or ones you need right now can, of course, be kept with confidence. When you're left with only those books that you love, you'll discover that the quality of information you receive changes noticeably. The room you make by discarding books seems to create space for an equivalent volume of new information. You'll soon see that the information you need comes just when you need it, and when it does, you'll find that you respond to it immediately in a new pattern of behaviour that wasn't possible when you were hoarding books and neglecting the information they contained.

As with clothing, you must begin by taking every single book you own off the shelves and piling them on the floor. Then take them in your hands and keep only

those that spark joy. Whatever you do, don't start reading them. If you have too many books to choose all at once, sort them by categories, such as general (for reading), practical (references, cookbooks), visual (coffee-table books) and magazines, and do the joy check for each category.

## Series

Manga, comic books and other series are normally tidied up under the category of 'general books', but if you have a large volume, make this a separate category. When dealing with a series, it isn't necessary to hold each one in your hands. You can check whether or not they spark joy by piling the whole series together and putting your arms around the pile as though hugging it, or by just taking the top volume in your hands.

The risk for distraction with this category is extremely high. To avoid wasting the entire day reading them, the trick is never to open them. Check for joy by simply touching them. During private lessons, if I make the mistake of mentioning my clients' manga, they are quite likely to launch into a long and passionate explanation of the series' charms.

# Magazines and coffee-table books

Books that have a strong element of being 'fun to look at' include not only magazines and photo books but also catalogues, art books and the like. Keep with confidence those that belong in your personal Hall of Fame, that is, those you would not even contemplate discarding and that you know without a doubt spark joy. Magazines are short-distance runners with a very brief 'season'. If the magazines you buy regularly or to which you subscribe tend to accumulate, I suggest setting a limit on the maximum number of issues that you can keep.

If you are only attracted to certain photos or articles in a book, cut those out. You do not have to put them in a scrapbook right away. Store them temporarily in a clear plastic folder. It's quite common for people to look at these clips later and wonder why they kept them, so sort through these once again when you get to the paper sorting stage.

# Storing books attractively

I have my clients store their books in a bookcase or on a set of shelves placed out of sight in the wardrobe, in a storage room or in a cupboard. The basic rule is to keep items of the same category together, but for books that are used in a specific place, it is fine to keep them where they are used, such as storing cookbooks in the kitchen. Don't stack them in a pile. Be sure to stand them up.

After you've finished tidying your books, you may wonder whether you should have kept so many, but don't worry. As you continue tidying, you will hone your sensitivity to joy. If you notice anything later on that has served its purpose, you can discard it at that time. And it's such a pleasure to have lots of books that spark joy. If you have picked them up one by one and determined that these are indeed the books you love, then keep them with confidence and make up your mind to cherish them.

## BECOMING A PERSON WHO MATCHES
## THE BOOKS YOU'VE KEPT

When you've finished tidying your books, step back and take a good look at your bookshelves. What kinds of words leap out at you from the titles on their spines? If you have been telling everyone you'd like to get married sometime this year, but you have a lot of titles with words like 'XXX for Singles', or if you want to live a joyful life but own a lot of novels with tragic titles, watch out.

The energy of book titles and the words inside them are very powerful. In Japan, we say that 'words make our reality'. The words we see and with which we come into contact tend to bring about events of the same nature. In that sense, you will become the person who matches the books you have kept. What kind of books would you want in your bookcase to reflect the kind of person you aspire to be? If you choose which books to keep on that basis, you may find that the course of events in your life changes dramatically.

# 6

# Tidying papers

## The basic rule for papers:
## Discard everything

L ike clothes and books, the first step in tidying papers is to gather all the documents and papers for which you are personally responsible in one place. My rule of thumb? Discard everything.

This does not mean that the goal is to discard every single one. Rather, it means that you should choose from among them on the premise that they will be recycled. A single sheet of paper takes up almost no room, which makes it very easy to accumulate far too many before you realize it. If you don't approach the selection process with a commitment to getting rid of them all, you will barely make a dent in the overall volume. Keep only those for which there is a clear purpose – those you are currently using, those you will need for a limited period and those that you need to keep indefinitely.

It's important to check each one. If there is a stack of papers in an envelope, remove them all because there may be unnecessary papers, such as advertising leaflets, mixed in with essential ones. Sorting papers can give you a headache, so keep yourself hydrated and plough steadily through each category.

## Make a pending box

One essential item for tidying papers is a 'pending' box. Place all those papers that require action, such as letters you are planning to send, outstanding bills, etc., in this box, and forge ahead with tidying. Anything that can be dealt with immediately, however, such as checking what's inside an envelope or glancing through a pamphlet so that you can recycle it, should be handled on the spot. If you accumulate too many papers that are pending, you will be reluctant to deal with them later.

In general, a magazine holder in which papers can be stood upright makes a good pending box, but you can also use an empty box, if you have one of an appropriate size, or a clear plastic folder if the volume of documents and papers is minimal.

If you are undertaking your tidying campaign with the whole family, make sure you have only one pending box for each person.

## Course materials

Do you have materials from courses you took for career development or to obtain degrees? Or perhaps you've kept materials from a seminar for personal development. People tend to save these in the hope that someday they'll be able to review them; but, tell me, have you ever done so? In most cases, 'someday' never comes.

These courses have value while they are being taken, but they only have meaning when you put what you learned through them into practice. I believe that hanging on to such materials actually prevents us from using what we've learned. When you take such courses, resolve to recycle the materials when you're done. If you regret having done so, take the course again, and this time apply what you learn right away.

# Credit card statements

Credit card statements rank at the top of the list for papers that people tend to hang on to. As these statements are sent monthly, if you have more than one card, they add up quickly.

Yet for most of us, they are really just information about how much we've spent. Once you've confirmed the content and recorded everything in your household accounts, their job is done. Unless you need them for year-end income tax, put them through the shredder. Many credit card companies provide very convenient electronic statement services, and it might be worthwhile to switch over to that.

# Warranties

Every electrical appliance you buy comes with a warranty. This is the most common document found in every home, and many people tend to save them properly

by storing them in a folder file or in an accordion-style file. But having many compartments is actually the greatest drawback of this type of filing system. Once your warranties are each tucked into their own compartment, you are unlikely to look at them again, and, before you realize it, you will have files full of expired warranties.

The simplest storage solution is to keep all of them in a single clear plastic folder. Every time you search through this folder for a warranty, it gives you a chance to see all the others and weed out any that have expired. If you need proof of purchase, store the receipt with the relevant warranty.

## Manuals

In addition to being both boring and difficult to read, manuals are hefty tomes that take up a lot of room. Most people would rather not keep them but feel obliged to. It is quite common to carefully save them even when the appliances to which they belong have long since broken down and been replaced. Rest assured. You can recycle them all.

Even if you find you need a manual after you have gotten rid of it, the information can be found online or by calling the manufacturer. If, however, you are one of those people who gets a thrill out of manuals or who frequently consults their camera guide, go through them carefully and select the ones that you particularly love.

# Greeting cards

Greeting cards are one of the hardest things in this category to discard. They carry special messages from friends or family and may have a photo on the front, which can make them seem like sentimental items.

The main purpose of a greeting card, however, is to convey a greeting. The moment you finish reading it, its job is done. Keep only those that truly spark joy.

# Clippings

Recipe clippings that you've hung on your fridge but never made, tourist maps of places you have no plans to visit, newspaper articles you intended to read that are now out of date ... do any of these things spark joy for you now?

I once had a habit of cutting out maps of Kyoto and Kamakura whenever I came across them in magazines, but when I visited those cities, I always forgot to take the clippings. In the end, I tossed them all!

For any clippings that you decide to keep, a display book with clear plastic pockets is a simple solution that is easy to flip through. If you want to increase the joy factor, a good alternative is to make your own personal scrapbook. Clippings that don't really need to be filed, such as an article on a shop you plan to visit soon, however, should be kept in the pending box or in your datebook.

# Assign a day to attend to pending items

Once you've finished tidying up your papers, check the contents of your pending box. Is it full? When it comes to pending papers, it's best to set aside a specific time and deal with them in one fell swoop. Ones that can be recycled once you've checked the contents should be dealt with immediately. Powered by that momentum, move on to tackle those that require a response or some other action.

It is possible to tackle the contents of your pending box after you have finished your entire tidying campaign, but things that are pending weigh on the mind far more than you might expect. You will have much greater peace of mind if you deal with them before you start tidying your *komono*.

## HOW TO TIDY PAPERS AT THE OFFICE

If you are tidying up your office, the basic rule is to start with your own desk before you tackle any communal spaces. Tidy up in one go, just as you would at home. The basic order for tidying is books, papers, stationery goods and, finally, other *komono*.

If you have an average-size desk, it will take you a total of six hours. I recommend undertaking your tidying campaign early in the morning when almost no one is there, which would require three two-hour sessions, but if you are able to find a whole six hours to work on it at a stretch, one session will be enough.

It would be a shame to give up because you were too busy to spend six hours on tidying. According to certain statistical data, the average person spends about thirty minutes a day searching for things, while people who misplace a lot can spend as much as two hours a day. If a person works twenty days a month, this means he or she is wasting up to forty hours a month just looking for things. If you can solve this problem in a mere six hours, the return on your time investment will be both dramatic and immediate. With a tidy desk that brings you joy, your work efficiency is bound to increase!

# 7
# Tidying *komono*

hen it comes to deciding where to store things, *komono* (miscellaneous items) is the most difficult category because it has such an overwhelming number of subcategories. Stationery supplies, electrical cords, cosmetics, kitchen goods, food, cleaning supplies, laundry items . . . it's enough to make your head spin just thinking about it. I also once struggled to decide where to keep my *komono*. Just thinking about it made me feel feverish, and the sight of all the *komono* spread out before me made me want to give up. I would crawl into bed and wish that some little elves would come in and put everything away for me while I slept. When I awoke, however, I was faced with the undeniable truth that nothing had changed. I don't know how many times I gave up hope as I stood before my storage shelves. But don't worry.

The key to fast and efficient *komono* tidying is to know your categories. Once you've identified the categories that exist in your home, you can follow the three basic steps for each one:

1. Gather all items in that category in one place.
2. Choose only those that spark joy.
3. Store by category.

There may be some *komono* categories that you share with other members of your family, but the policy is to start with those that belong to you alone. If you live by yourself, you can start with any *komono* category you like.

If you come across *komono* that don't particularly spark joy yet are necessary, try praising them to the hilt. Think of how they make your life easier, about their wonderful appearance and marvellous features, and tell them how great they are. As you do this, you will begin to feel grateful for how they help you and to see how they support your life. They will no longer be simply something convenient to have, and you will gradually begin to feel a thrill of joy when you see them. If you cannot find anything to praise, or if it feels unnatural to praise an item, then follow the prompting of your heart.

Tidying *komono* is a terrific opportunity to hone your sensitivity to joy. Your possessions contribute so much to your daily life, so try communing with them properly, with gratitude.

# CDs and DVDs

While the order of tidying *komono* categories is up to you, most people tackle CDs and DVDs first. This can make it easier to choose which ones spark joy because, as information sources, CDs and DVDs are similar to books and papers. As usual, gather them all in one spot, pick each one up, and keep only those that spark joy. If you have any items that you plan to get rid of once you've uploaded or installed them into your computer, put them in the pending box you made when tidying papers. If you love the jackets and just having them makes you happy, keep them as they are.

You may come across sentimental CDs from friends or lovers, but if these just remind you of a time when you listened to such music, enjoy the nostalgia of that memory, discard the CD with thanks and move on to the next one! Whatever you do, don't stop to listen to music or watch a DVD.

# Stationery supplies

Stationery supplies can be subdivided into equipment, paper-related supplies, and letter-writing supplies.

## Equipment

Let's start with equipment. This covers things that usually do not diminish in volume, such as pens, scissors, staplers and rulers. Any pens that haven't been used for some time should be checked to see if they still write. This is the time to discard those that don't spark joy, including any received as promotional giveaways.

This is a diverse category characterized by a broad range of tools made of a wide variety of materials. Divide them into snug, well-defined compartments, and store them vertically. Small items, such as boxes of staples, rubbers and mechanical pencil leads, will feel more secure if you keep them in smaller boxes, such as those for rings.

## Paper-related supplies

Paper–related stationery supplies include items made of paper, such as notebooks, memo pads, Post–its, and files, as well as goods used to store papers, such as clear plastic folders and binders.

Do you have dozens of notebooks that are still half blank? When people start a new project, it's natural to want to use a new notebook. Discard all those that have finished their purpose unless they spark joy.

Don't forget to tidy up your clear plastic folders. This is one of the most easily accumulated items, and the record holder among my clients owned 420. She ended up donating them to her company.

It is standard practice to store paper–related stationery supplies next to documents and papers, because they are, after all, made of the same material. Small items, such as memo pads and Post–its can be stood upright in a small box, which can then be placed on a shelf for a neater appearance.

## Letter-writing supplies

Stationery supplies for writing letters are just what the name implies: letter papers, envelopes, postcards and the like. You can tidy any other items needed for writing letters at the same time, such as stamps and address labels.

I once aspired to be a good letter writer who wrote prompt and proper thank-you letters. I accumulated numerous letter sets, but I almost always missed the opportunity to send a letter and ended up thanking people by email. If your letter set doesn't spark joy, you won't be motivated to write a letter. The iron rule is to keep only those letter-writing supplies that inspire you to write. You are bound to come across things like postcards bought on the spur of the moment while travelling that you now wonder why on earth you bought. If their spark is gone, thank them for the memory and recycle them, but be sure to keep any with designs that you really love even if you are never going to send them.

# Electrical *komono*

Electrical *komono* cover such items as digital cameras, portable game players and computers. If, however, your hobby is cameras, for example, and you have a large volume of camera parts, you can make this a separate category and tackle it later.

Many people tend to hoard old mobile phones. One of my clients had a total of seventeen. If you have a sentimental attachment to your mobile phones that makes them hard to discard, leave them for when you sort your sentimental items category. If you want the photo data, put the phone in your pending box, and don't forget to deal with those photos later on! When disposing of mobile phones and computers, you can take advantage of the collection services offered by electrical appliance stores and electronics recycling organizations.

## Electrical cords

Cords are the most typical electrical *komono*, and they are often a tangled mess. Do you have any surplus chargers lying around? And how about those earphones that came with something you no longer remember? Do you really need them?

Remove these kinds of cords from any plastic bags you've stored them in, untangle the whole mess and pick each one up to check for joy. As you do this, you are guaranteed to come across cords that you cannot identify. These mystery cords should not be saved for later, but rather should be dealt with on the spot. If you have finished tidying your electrical appliances, the job of matching each cord to an appliance will be far simpler. Any mystery cords that remain should be recycled guilt-free.

## Memory cards and batteries

When I use the term 'electrical', I mean things that seem to 'smell' electric. Electrical things exude a sort of pungent, tingling odour, so search out the remaining electrical *komono* using this sensation as your guide.

In addition to memory cards, USBs, empty DVD disks, printer ink cartridges, and batteries, you can also tidy up any electrical health and beauty devices as part of this category. When I visit homes that have multiple cords springing from the outlets or an abundance of electrical appliances, the air in the entranceway has what feels like an electrical charge. Perhaps that sensation transmits itself to our bodies, because once these things are completely tidied up, there is – surprise, surprise – a physical sense of relief.

# Skincare products and cosmetics

Skincare products are water based and therefore freshness is essential. The secret to increasing the joy of caring for your skin is to use up your skincare supplies before they expire. If you keep skincare samples on hand for when you travel, ask yourself honestly whether you have ever taken them with you on a trip. If the samples are the same as the products you already use, then one solution is to open them up and add them to the bottle you are already using.

If you have skincare products that you don't use but still find hard to part with, don't put them away. Instead, use them lavishly on your body.

The standard storage place for skincare supplies is near the bathroom sink for ease of use. If you only have a few, it is simplest to store them all together in one spot.

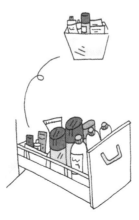

Small items, such as samples, tubes of eye cream, and so on, can be stored neatly in a smallish box. If there's not enough space, you can make a special corner for them in your wardrobe or on a shelf where you keep *komono*. If you have too many to store in one place, you can divide them into items used daily and those used less frequently.

## Makeup

Keep in mind that skincare products and makeup should always be kept separately. Contrary to what many people think, skincare products are not makeup. From my perspective, it's the nature of the two that differs. Skin lotions and creams are moist and watery, whereas many makeup products, such as powders and shiny brushes, repel water. Exposure to the moisture in skincare products can actually compromise the quality of a cosmetic. A single drop of skin lotion falling into your blush, for example, could ruin it. That's why it's best to store your makeup and skincare products separately. In many instances, they may need to be stored in the same drawer, but it will be safer if you clearly separate them by putting your skincare products in their own box. You can then remove them, box and all, and take them to a different place to use them.

Products that seem to fall into both categories, such as a liquid base coat that also serves as a skin lotion, can be stored with either one, as can hair care products.

Perfumes are best stored either as open displays like accessories or near your makeup items.

When tidying makeup, it's best to be strict when selecting what to keep. Now is the time to say goodbye to any old cosmetics or ones that no longer suit your taste.

Cosmetics take delight in a pretty space. The approach I use for makeup is the same as that for accessories: I store them in a box in a drawer or in a makeup box or makeup bag. If you have a dressing table, this is where your cosmetics belong. Having a dressing table is a strength. Fewer than 30 per cent of my clients have them, and I have only met one who knew how to maximize the beauty of it. Usually the opposite is true.

Take client M, for example. When I first entered her room, her slim wooden dressing table seemed so chaotic that it took me a moment to recognize what it was. Makeup implements were strewn across the top – a bottle of liquid foundation with a dribble of beige liquid oozing down the side, a powder compact with a cracked lid, blush and eye shadow compacts with their lids gaping open. Various brushes sprawled randomly nearby. Nail files and lipsticks protruded like pegs from the shallow top drawer, preventing it from shutting. And over all lay a film of fine dust, as if my client had sifted powdered sugar over the top. It resembled a haunted house more than a dressing table.

You would think that people who own a dressing table want it to look beautiful, yet in many cases my clients have turned them into a parking lot for their cosmetics. I don't own a lot of cosmetics and am a complete amateur when it comes to wearing makeup. Curious to see if there were any storage points that are specific to makeup, I had been contemplating going to the cosmetic section of a department store to interview the staff or asking a friend who was good at makeup when S came to seek my advice. This was perfect timing. S is a professional makeup artist. In addition to giving courses on the subject, she has also worked at the Paris Collection and as a makeup specialist for celebrities. She now has her own beauty salon where she provides personalized instruction.

The way she stores her cosmetics and tools is exactly what you would expect of a professional. When I visited her home, she had just given her dressing table to a friend, and instead she had stored her makeup in a plain square box along with a folding mirror. Inside, the cosmetics were expertly divided into foundations, eyelashes, eye shadows and liners, lipsticks and glosses and blushes. All the parts and tools were also divided by category. Whenever possible, items were stored standing, and the contents were arranged so that every item was visible at a glance.

'I've divided everything into teams. Team 1 consists of the things I use daily, and Team 2 are the things I keep on hand to add variation. Team 1 has all the things I need to make my basic look complete, and I keep it in a pouch that I take with me for touchups whenever I need one,' she told me. 'If putting on your makeup is too much work, it's game over. The basic rule for storing makeup is to eliminate every unnecessary step.'

She also kept cotton buds in a business card case, and removed eye shadows from their cases to make her own original palette. 'Dirty cosmetic containers are pretty gross. You should wipe any cases that contain powders frequently to keep them clean. If you don't, beauty will slip further and further away.

'As for shelf life, powders will keep two or three years once they've been opened. Get rid of lipsticks after about a year, when they start smelling oily. Things like liquid foundation, which are more like skincare products, only last about a year, too.' From the perspective of a professional, the life of cosmetics was much shorter than I had expected. In my work, many of the ones I come across have easily been around for five years or more.

'There's no rule that says you have to put on makeup, right? That means if you want to wear makeup, you need to keep your motivation up. So it's worth getting some items that increase your motivation. The joy factor is especially important for anything related to cosmetics. After all, makeup is part of the ritual that prepares you for your day. If you aren't feeling joy about your morning routine, then that's the kind of day you're going to have.'

S had quickly turned my lesson on storage into a lecture on makeup, but one that gave me two precious insights. The first was that makeup storage must be really easy to grasp. Precisely because there are so many items in this category, it's crucial to be able to tell at a glance where they are. The best way is to store individual components separately, like S did. To do this, compartments are essential, and therefore, it's best to either use a makeup box with many small compartments, just like professional makeup artists do, or find the right kind of empty boxes or storage units.

You may be like me and not have enough cosmetics to make it worth using a lot of compartments. In that case, the simplest approach is to divide your makeup and equipment into things that can be stored standing and things that can't. Find a container that can hold all the equipment that stands up. It could be a tube-shaped can, a glass cup, or anything else that works. Use this for sticklike items, such as mascara, eyeliner, and brushes. The other items can just be stored together normally in something like a pouch or a box. Even here, you can store powder compacts and eye shadow palettes standing up to save space. But if you have enough room, it's easier to see the colours and enhance the joy factor if you store them flat, so adjust the storage to suit your own taste.

# Relaxation goods

In the last few years, I have noticed a steady increase in the average number of aromatherapy–related items people own, such as candles and oils, which is perhaps an indication that more people seek relaxation and healing. Check every item in this category to see if it sparks joy, including massage and acupressure items. Discard old aroma oils or fragrances that no longer appeal. Make sure when you store them that your relaxation goods can also relax. You can increase the relaxation effect significantly by selecting a container made of natural material such as rattan and by using dividers.

# Medicines

Medicine somehow seems like it should last forever, but this is not the case. You are bound to have some in your medicine chest that are long past the expiration date. I once found a bottle of Seirogan (the Japanese version of Pepto-Bismol) that was over twenty years old, and the smell was shocking. Discard expired medicines as well as any undated medicines for which you no longer remember getting a prescription.

The most common approach to storage is to stand them upright in your medicine chest, but if you only have a small amount, you can store them very simply by putting them all in a pouch.

# Valuables

Hands on her hips, my client gazes at the *komono* inundating the room and sighs. 'KonMari, I know you said I should store things by material and I can pretty much identify cloth, paper, and electric things, but how am I supposed to identify the other stuff?'

'Smell them,' I tell her.

There is an awkward silence as she stares at me.

'Close your eyes,' I say. One at a time, I hold three items under her nose for about ten seconds each. Then I ask, 'What did they smell like?'

'Well . . . hmmm . . . I don't know why but somehow they smell like money.' She sounds uncertain, but she is absolutely right. The three items were a chequebook, a 10,000 yen note and a gift certificate. Things that fall into the 'valuables' category, such as cash, credit cards, and coupons are essentially 'money'. There is something about them that gives off the same dense metallic aroma. It might be easiest to get an image if you think of the smell of newly minted coins.

Interestingly, while information items such as books and documents are also made of paper, just like chequebooks and money, the former have a slightly acidic smell while the latter have an astringent smell, a bit like iron. Wondering if this difference was related to the concept of yin–yang and the five elements, I checked a feng shui book and discovered that books fall under the element of wood, while money falls under metal. In another reference material, I found that with regard to the sense of taste, wood is classified as sour, while money is classified as bitter. These qualities might simply be related to different physical characteristics, such as the type of ink used or the odour of mildew that accrues when books are piled on top of each other, but it still made me happy to see that my intuition agreed with this ancient wisdom.

Some people don't discern distinct differences in smell the way I do, but the harder a client has worked to reduce, the more likely he or she is to nod in agreement. The aura your things emit will change depending on their role in your life, on how they are treated and on the characteristics of the materials from which they are made. They may not actually have any odour, but it seems to be my sense of smell that registers the difference. The human senses have powers that cannot always be explained by logic.

Valuables are the one category where practicality, not the joy factor, takes priority when selecting what to keep. Discard any items that have expired, and put those you wish to use or deposit in your pending box and set a date for getting this done.

Because they are valuable, they have a fair bit of pride and should be stored with respect in something like a dresser drawer or a wooden box. For storing cards, I recommend using boxes the size of those that contain business cards. Any cards that you don't normally carry with you, such as backup credit cards, medical cards, etc., can be stored in the plastic pockets of a card case, but they're easier to remove if you store them standing up in a box, which makes this storage method more efficient. Things like a wallet or purse you usually use when travelling, foreign currency and your passport also fall into this subcategory.

Among all the things that fall within the subcategory of valuables, the wallet is like a king to whom you can never show too much respect. Strictly speaking, it is really money that should be treated with respect, but naked money left exposed is vulnerable. If you take a hundred-dollar bill and place it on the table, it loses any hint of its former

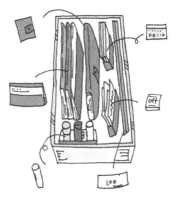

majesty. Instead, it looks very forlorn and embarrassed at being caught off guard. But as soon as you put it in your wallet or purse, it regains its pride and emanates authority.

Wallets and purses, however, tire easily. Money is used quite roughly. It is your wallet that willingly embraces money with all its emotional baggage. To support your wallet in its service as a receptacle, you should set aside a place for it to rest. This doesn't mean that you have to do anything complicated. Like all your other possessions, you just need to find it the right home. **By taking good care of your wallet, you will feel gratitude every time you remove some cash, and this will actually change how you use your money.** Oftentimes I hear a client say, 'I feel so grateful now when I take money out of my purse. It makes it possible for me to eat three meals a day and buy the things that bring me joy. This habit has really altered the way I spend.'

## Sewing kits

Let me ask you a question. How often do you use your sewing kit? Many people respond that they have barely touched it for a year and some are still using the same one they got in school. Is there anything in your sewing kit that you know you will never use but have just left there anyway? You may, for example, have accumulated multiple thimbles or tailor's chalk, or still have scraps of felt from something you made a long time ago. This is also the time to deal with those buttons you were intending to sew on but never got around to.

## Tools

In addition to screwdrivers, hammers and saws, this category also includes nails and screws, as well as the hexagonal wrench or casters that came with the furniture you bought and bolts for which the application is unclear. Check them to see which ones you need and keep only those that are essential.

Tools are very tough by nature, and therefore they need no detailed rules for storage. Once you've gathered them together, store them in an empty space. I reduced mine to the bare minimum, which I keep in a leftover pouch on a shelf.

## Hobby *komono*

To pursue an interest such as flower arranging, calligraphy or hula dancing, people often take lessons, and many of these pastimes require special equipment. If you pursue only a single interest, such as calligraphy, assign one storage place for everything related to it. Even if you have many interests, you can designate a single storage space for hobby-related *komono*. If you have equipment from activities you no longer pursue and that no longer spark joy, now is the time to part with it. You will be surprised at how much lighter you feel.

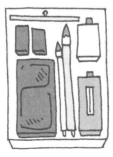

# Collectibles

Collectibles include figurines, fan club paraphernalia, items with a specific theme, or any other thing you collect for no reason except that you simply can't resist. Have you left any such items in their packages and stuffed them into a cardboard box as if they didn't spark joy?

Tidying items you collect is time-consuming, so the most important rule is to make sure you set aside enough time. Be prepared to commit a whole day. Use the same basic approach. Gather everything together in one spot, then take each one in your hands and see whether or not it sparks joy. At first you may think, 'I couldn't possibly throw this away,' but if you pick it up again, you are bound to find more than one that you may be finished with. Once you have decided which to keep, divide them into your own personal categories and make them into a display that sparks joy.

# Things you kept 'just because'

This *komono* category consists of things that you've kept without really knowing why, such as metal parts you never used that came with a wristwatch, hair pins that you removed and just left lying around, spare buttons, old mobile phone cases and random keychains. You will likely be discarding almost all of them. Store any that you do keep near things that seem similar in nature. For example, hair pins would belong with hair accessories, and buttons would belong with sewing equipment. Once they have a home and companions, things that formerly seemed lost without a fixed address regain their shine.

# Linen and bedding

If you live with your family or just happen to have a large amount of linen, treat it as a *komono* category. To check for joy, don't just touch it. Smell it! Linen that isn't used very often tends to absorb odours to a surprising degree. And whatever you do, don't leave sheets or pillowcases in their packages unopened because the plastic wrapping traps moisture. I can't tell you how many sheets I've come across in my career that have mildewed because they weren't removed from the bag. If you have any, I urge you to take them out of their packages right now and start using them to prevent such a tragedy.

Tidy not only blankets and pillows but also your cushions when tackling bedding. Throw away any that no longer spark joy because they have become worn and tattered or that you have not used for a year. Once you've checked your own bedding, check any you keep for company. In traditional Japanese homes, all bedding, which consists of futon mattresses, sheets, blankets and quilts, is stored in the wardrobe. As bedding for guests is not taken out of the wardrobe very often and Japan is a humid country, my clients quite often find that guest bedding has become mildewed.

## Towels

A cupboard in or near the bathroom is the most standard storage place for towels, but if you don't have room, try storing them in a drawer in your wardrobe. Even those towels that you are planning to use as rags and then dispose of should be folded and stored upright, not stuffed in a bag. This allows you to see how many you have and avoid overstocking.

# Stuffed toys

One of the most common sentimental items is stuffed toys, and they win hands down at being one of the hardest to discard. As a teenager, during the period when I was obsessed with tidying to the point that I was virtually a discarding machine, I could not bring myself to throw away a particular stuffed animal – Koro-chan, a brown Chow Chow that I got when I was little and that was as big as me at the time. I had always wanted a dog and treated him just like a pet. I would feed him with a bowl full of marbles, which I called dog food. When I was in elementary school, I liked to sit on him and tell him all about my day. But as time went on, I played with him less and less, until finally he was relegated to a spot beside the TV, where I almost never touched him.

After about a year, I began to get the sniffles whenever I was in the house. In my line of work, dust flies constantly, yet it never bothers me. At that time, however, I had an allergy to animal fur. Whenever I was exposed, my nose would start itching immediately. The only pets we kept at home, however, were guppies. What, I wondered, could be causing my runny nose?

'Maybe it's Koro-chan,' my mother suggested.

I looked at my stuffed dog and suddenly noticed that he was pretty dusty. The weight of his body had caused his front paws to splay and his head had sunk to the floor, making him a great dust collector. 'I guess we'll have to get rid of him. You have lots of other stuffed toys anyway,' my parents said, but I refused to let them take him away. I cleaned him with the vacuum cleaner and put him out in the sun, but nothing seemed to help. My nose kept on running, and in the end I had no choice but to let him go. My father and I placed him in a plastic bag. Standing in front of it, we pressed our hands together and bowed. 'Thank you for everything,' we said, and carried him to the garbage bin. It was all over in moments, but that was the first time in my life that I had ever felt so ambivalent about throwing something away.

I always thank my things when I discard them, but I treat things like stuffed animals that seem to have a soul with extra respect, as if conducting a memorial service. The reason stuffed animals and dolls are so hard to throw away is because they seem to be alive. I think it's because of their eyes, which appear to follow us. I can't tell you how many times I have heard my clients say, 'I put all my stuffed animals in a plastic bag, but their eyes seemed to plead with me, and in the end, I just had to take them out again.' And it's no wonder. I can still remember Koro-chan's imploring eyes looking at me through that plastic bag.

Energy resides in the eyes, which is why it's best to cover them when discarding something. Once their eyes are hidden, stuffed toys and dolls look much more like objects, and that makes it far easier to part with them. The simplest solution is to place a cloth or piece of paper over their faces. One of my clients had a toy cat with a T-shirt, and we pulled the T-shirt up to cover its face. The result was quite comical, allowing my client to part with it cheerfully.

If it still bothers you, try the Japanese purification rite of throwing in some coarse salt to send the spirits on their way. If you find it hard to let something go, approaching the parting as a kind of memorial service can help reduce your ambivalence. Incidentally, a temple in Japan that conducts memorial services for dolls covers their faces with cloth to keep them clean and also ties up their hair, so my suggestions would appear to follow proper etiquette.

# Recreational items

Recreational items come in all sizes, from picnic baskets, badminton sets and balls, to skis, snowboards and fishing gear. Keep with confidence any that bring you joy, even if you don't use them that frequently or if it's just the sight of them that makes you happy. If you store recreational items in plastic bags, they will look like garbage, and you will use them far less often than you otherwise might. If you must keep them in a bag, make it one that you really like.

# Seasonal items

Seasonal items include large things such as artificial Christmas trees or small items such as holiday ornaments and decorations. Keep only those that you really want to display next season. These should be stored by theme. To prevent overlooking them when their season rolls around, label the box or drawer in which you store them. Start displaying those that are in season right away.

# Emergency supplies

Your tidying campaign is the perfect time to do an overall check of the supplies you keep on hand for emergencies and disasters, such as helmets, earthquake survival kits, flashlights, radio, portable toilet and so on.

Do you have food rations or medical supplies that have expired or a radio that no longer works? While sorting this category, many people discover disaster mitigation goods that they haven't gotten around to using, such as anchors that prevent furniture from toppling in an earthquake. If you find any of these, use them now. Survival kits are usually kept near the entrance, such as the hall closet. Be sure that all family members know where they are.

# Rain gear

If you have an umbrella for each member of your household, that should be plenty. Watch out for plastic umbrellas, which tend to pile up. As time passes, the plastic sticks together and yellows, so open them up to make sure they are still usable. One of my clients who lived alone had twenty-two umbrellas. Unfortunately, she had to throw almost all of them away. After tidying your umbrellas, you can also tackle other rain gear.

# Kitchen *komono*

H lived in a three-bedroom apartment with her husband and two daughters. 'My kitchen is such a mess it's hard to use,' she told me. She led me into a kitchen that was about two metres square. If I were to describe it in one word, that word would be 'grey'.

The breakfast dishes were still piled in the sink. A bottle of dish soap and a sodden sponge sat on a wire rack fastened with a sucker pad beside the tap. To the right, a large dish rack occupied more than half the counter space. It was so full of dishes you would have thought H had just had a party. 'My dish rack is now the dish cupboard,' she said with a laugh. Successive layers of water marks covered the sink, making it look almost white.

I shifted my eyes to the stove. She seemed to be storing her frying pan on one of the burners for lack of anywhere else to put it, and a wire stand beside the range was jammed full of spice bottles. Bottles of soy sauce, cooking wine and other ingredients were lined up in front of it. An aluminium shield, whose job was to catch oil splatters behind the stove, was so sticky with grease it seemed to be shouting, 'Stop!'

'It just looks so lived in,' H said. 'I want to really clear things out.' It was all she could manage to make the meals, she told me. Putting things away seemed like such a chore, and just standing in the kitchen made her want to despair.

I don't believe that kitchens have to be perfectly tidy

all the time, nor do I have anything against kitchens that look lived in. **All you need is a kitchen in which you can enjoy cooking**. In good ramen shops, for example, the kitchen may look like a disaster, but the food still tastes great as long as the chef takes pride in making the best noodles.

What type of kitchen is a joy to cook in? My clients' answers are usually, 'A kitchen that's always clean,' 'One where everything I need is right at hand,' or 'A place where I can wear my favourite apron and use my favourite pots and pans.' The latter can be achieved by going out and buying things you like, so we'll ignore it for the moment, and the first one relates to cleaning, not tidying. The only one for which tidying might provide a solution is the second one – having everything easily at hand. But this is actually a big misunderstanding.

I used to be obsessed with finding the best way of storing things in the kitchen for handy access to cooking tools. I read every magazine feature on kitchen layout I could find, attached hooks to the wall and hung my pans and equipment from them. I simulated cooking, measuring the distance from my arm to each location to determine the best place for my seasonings. In the end, this meant that I kept everything out on the counter instead of storing things in the cupboard. While it was indeed easier to reach things, oil and water splattered everywhere, leaving a greasy film over the entire kitchen and totally eliminating any joy I might have felt when cooking.

## Ease of cleaning is the criterion for kitchen storage

Wondering where this idea that the ideal kitchen is one where everything is within reach comes from, I asked people. Almost everyone I talked to was imagining a kitchen in a restaurant or café. To investigate the secrets of such a kitchen, I got permission to observe a restaurant kitchen between the lunch and dinner hours. Donning an apron and cap and armed with my camera and trusty notebook, I entered full of anticipation, expecting to discover the tricks of the trade. But I was disappointed. Other than the standard method of storing everything in the stainless steel kitchen by category, such as dishes, pots, pans and cooking utensils, there was not one storage trick to be seen.

When I thought about it, I realized that in restaurants, the type of cuisine that is served, whether Japanese or Italian, pretty much determines the seasonings and cooking utensils required, and therefore, the amount of things stored in the kitchen will never increase. In addition, restaurant kitchens are designed for a completely different purpose than those in regular homes, with many open shelves near the ceiling and on the walls.

I was just thinking to myself that my visit to the restaurant had been a waste of time when the chefs returned to prepare for the dinner shift. I stepped out of the way and watched them absently as they worked, when suddenly I noticed a crucial point. The cooks moved quickly and efficiently the entire time, but their speed and efficiency was most noticeable not when they were actually cooking, but whenever they stopped to wipe down the sink or counter. They ran a cloth over those areas every time they used them, and when they finished with a frying pan, they scrubbed the oil off with a long-handled brush. At the end of the day, they wiped down every surface, including not only the stove top and counters, but also the walls. When I asked the head chef what the secret of tidying a kitchen was, he replied, 'Tidying the kitchen means wiping away any water and oil.'

After that, I observed the kitchens in several other restaurants, but they were all the same. **The focus was not on ease of use, but on ease of cleaning.** Once I realized this, I stopped trying to store things so that they would be easy to reach, and instead concentrated on storing everything, even dish soap and seasonings, in the cupboards. You might think that this would stuff your cupboards so full you couldn't get at the things you need, but never fear. It's true that when my clients' kitchens are tidied up, the cupboards are full to bursting while the counters are free of clutter. To get a frying pan, you have to slide it out from under a pile of other pots and pans, but when I ask my clients if this bothers them, they almost always respond, 'Actually, no. Doing this hasn't struck me as a bother even once.' Often they smile and add, 'In fact, I can't believe that I'm so conscientious about wiping the stove top every time I use it. It's not just that my kitchen is now *easy* to clean – I actually *want* to clean it.'

Oddly enough, when you are in a kitchen that is easy to clean, one that always looks spick-and-span, the effort of removing things from the cupboard doesn't seem stressful at all. If you want a kitchen that you can enjoy cooking in, aim for one that's easy to clean. The best way to do that is to make sure you put nothing on the counters or around the sink and stove top. You will be amazed at how easy your kitchen is to use if you design your storage with this aim in mind. Of course, if you happen to have a particularly large counter, you can keep things on an area that is free of splashing oil or water.

Perhaps some of you are thinking that only a person living alone could possibly succeed in keeping things off the counter, but half of my clients have children. Before we started, they were all sure that they could never keep their counter clear, but every one of them has succeeded. So I assure you, if you want to, you can.

My husband does a lot of the cooking, and whenever he's done, the kitchen is so clean it makes me wonder when he used it. It isn't because he cooks simply, either. Compared to my easy-to-clean, one-pot meal approach, his meals are quite complex. He'll serve an elaborate dish of fried tofu marinated in rice malt and sake and banana fried in coconut oil with balsamic sauce. When I asked him how he does it, he told me there are three secrets. He takes out all the implements and ingredients before he starts to reduce any unnecessary movement during the cooking process. He puts away each implement or ingredient as soon as he has finished with it. (This works very efficiently if you put away all the things in the same category at one time, just like for tidying up.) And finally, after cooking with oil, he immediately wipes everything down with hot water. If you like, try this method and see how it works.

This may sound counterintuitive, but I teach my clients to keep dish soaps and sponges away from the sink. Instead, we make a place for them in the cupboard underneath or on the inside of the cupboard door. This may seem like extra work, but if you try it, I'm sure you'll never again keep such things out on the counter.

Rarely do I come across a rubbish bin that brings anyone joy, so if possible let's store that under the sink as well. The only thing left to store now is the compost bin where you keep your kitchen scraps. Since the day I first left home, I have never kept my kitchen scraps out in a container. Consequently, my kitchen never smells like raw garbage. So what do I do with the kitchen scraps? I keep them in my freezer. I set aside a corner of the freezer for kitchen scraps and, after thoroughly draining them, I plop any fruit and vegetable peelings, chicken bones, etc., in a bag as I cook. Twice a week, on regular pickup days, I remove the bag of scraps.

I started doing this when I recalled that my mother froze the innards of the fish she gutted to keep the kitchen from smelling. While some people may cringe at the thought of putting kitchen scraps in the freezer with frozen foods, I freeze them before they begin to rot, so really they're just part of the food I eat, not garbage. If putting them in a compostable plastic bag looks unappealing to you, you can use a brown paper bag or a plastic container to separate your scrap corner even further.

## Tidying your kitchen first is a sure way to fail

'Forget about the rest. Just tell me how to store things in my kitchen!'

Have you ever felt like this? I'm sure at least some of you are thinking, 'That's me!' But people who want to do something about their kitchen first are almost always the ones who haven't yet managed to tidy even their clothes.

It's not a problem if, while you are in the process of tidying up your clothes, you start reducing things in the kitchen or reorganizing the kitchen drawers every time you use them. But in a proper tidying marathon, people who don't complete the process of selecting the things they love before working on kitchen storage almost always give up before they finish.

There are two reasons you should tidy up in order. The first one is related to our capacity to identify what brings us joy. If we don't hone that ability before we tackle kitchen *komono*, tragedy awaits. The subcategories within the kitchen *komono* category are many, and it takes time to tidy them up once and for all. It's very easy to get confused in the middle of this process, and when that happens, we can end up working at it for hours without getting anywhere, only to look up at two in the morning and, with sinking hearts, see an endless expanse of dishes, seasonings, pots and pans.

Unless we develop a solid sense of what brings us joy first through the process of tidying our clothes, then our books and papers, before we tackle kitchen *komono*, we will never reach the finish line of our tidying marathon. You may wonder how a ladle or a rice paddle can bring anyone joy, but if you have tidied your things in the right order and have begun to live a life in which you cherish the things you have left, you will be able to discern joy unerringly, even in things that appear to be merely utilitarian.

The second reason we need to tidy in the right order is because it eliminates wasteful purchases of unnecessary storage goods. The kitchen, which is full of implements of various sizes, requires the greatest volume of storage equipment per square foot. Yet almost none of my clients have to purchase extra storage units, because by the time they begin tidying their kitchen, they have enough spare dividers and drawers left over from reducing items in other categories.

Clear plastic cases used to store stationery supplies and wire racks used to store things in the wardrobe work so well under the sink it's as if they were made for that purpose. The blissful satisfaction that comes from seeing the storage in one's home balance out superbly in the end can only be understood when you have experienced it firsthand. It would be a waste to miss out on this pleasure because you had jumped the gun and bought new storage goods. Of course, if you have just moved out on your own, or if you don't have any storage goods or furniture, then you will need to buy some things. Also, once you've completed the tidying and storing process, you may decide you want to purchase ones that bring you more joy.

So how do you tidy up your kitchen? First, let me clarify: you aren't going to tidy your kitchen. You're going to tidy up the *komono* that belong in your kitchen. Tidy by category, not by location. Gather everything within the same category in one place and keep only those things that bring you joy.

**The three main categories of kitchen *komono* are implements for eating, cooking tools and food.** If you live alone, you can wait until you have finished sorting all three categories before storing them and store them all at once. If you live with a family and have a lot of kitchen *komono*, or if you have a proper dish cupboard, you have the option of starting by selecting which eating implements to keep and storing them in the dish cupboard, then moving on to cooking implements and food, which can be stored in the remaining spaces.

Here again, it's imperative to finish discarding first. Take everything that falls within the three main categories out of the kitchen cupboards and line them up so that you can finish the selection process properly. Once you have finished selecting what to keep and all your

## Eating implements

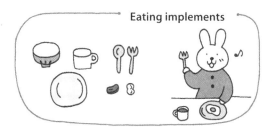

## Cooking tools

## Food

kitchen storage spaces have been emptied, store the items from each category together.

## Crockery

There were five members in my family, and our dish cupboard was always filled with dishes. The overflow spilled into the cupboards above the counter and the one beside the refrigerator, as well as half of the storage room in the hall. When I was a student, I felt so compelled to streamline our dish storage that I would get up at four in the morning and slip into the kitchen before my mother got up to cook. Still in my pyjamas, I would climb up onto the counter, peer inside the cupboards and rearrange the dishes, piling them differently each time, but without success. I even bought some storage goods so that I could stand them upright, just like *komono*, but this resulted in so much space between each dish that I could not fit them all back in the cupboard.

During this process, it occurred to me that people rarely take out one dish at a time if more than one person lives in the home. It's simply much more efficient to take out or put away a whole stack. Obviously, then, the problem with our house had to be the sheer volume of dishes. Going back to basics, I re-examined our cupboards and made some startling discoveries. First of all, we had enough dishes to run a cafeteria, yet we used the same ones every day. Not only that, but the ones we used on a daily basis were mostly 'rewards' that we had gotten on points, while all the expensive plates and tea sets received as gifts were carefully stored away in boxes as if they were precious treasures.

I immediately began pestering my mother. 'Look at this, Mum. Can't we take it out? I want to use it!' or 'If we're not going to use it, it's okay to get rid of it, right?' But she always brushed me off, saying, 'I've set it aside for a special occasion,' or 'I'm saving that for guests,' even though we had not entertained guests in our home for over a year.

In the end, I gave up without ever solving the problem of our dish cupboard cum warehouse, but it continued to puzzle me for years. When I began my current job, however, I was surprised to learn that my family was not unusual: the very same phenomenon occurred in many homes.

In the case of my clients, half-hearted sympathy just defeats the purpose. As the first step in tidying is to get rid of things that don't spark joy, I have my clients dispose of any dishes collected haphazardly and bring out the ones they have stored away for special occasions. While some are hesitant at first, anxious that they might break them, they soon discover how good it feels to use dishes they love every day. If you try it, you'll also realize that you don't break things that often. Besides, it will make the person who gave it to you much happier if you use it rather than leaving it in a box.

If you are still feeling reluctant to use good dishes on a daily basis, at least take the first step of unpacking them. While dishes used at specific times of year will probably be unpacked at least once a year even if stored out of sight, most dishes that are stored in boxes are never, ever used. I can also tell you from experience that there's a high probability that some sets you've put away in boxes don't spark joy. In addition, the boxes these dishes are packed in are usually filled with cardboard dividers and paper wrapping, which makes them a waste of space. It's quite common for my clients to find that, once they have unpacked these dishes and lined them up on their shelves, their dish cupboard looks neat and tidy, and they have plenty of space left over.

The empty boxes in which these dishes were packed make great storage items. For example, boxes made for sets of glasses are very sturdy and attractive, and work perfectly for storing many types of items upright, such as seasonings, dried foods, and noodles.

The real waste is insisting that it would be a waste to use beautiful gift sets. So make up your mind, once and for all: either use those dishes proudly or get rid of them.

Take a fresh look at every dish you own and see if it sparks joy. This may seem like a huge job if you own a lot of dishes, but look at it as a great chance to clean your whole dish cupboard! The basic approach to storage is to divide the cupboard into an area for dishes from which you drink, such as glasses, and an area for dishes from which you eat, such as plates, and then to stack dishes of similar shape.

After you have chosen the dishes that speak to your heart, it's time to store them. This can be done in one of two ways: you can either pile them on top of one another or add more shelves. In the average dish cupboard, it should be sufficient just to pile them. If the shelf is higher and you have space left over, you can add an extra shelf or use storage goods that add extra shelf space. A simple rack with legs or a wire rack with one or two shelves is the basic unit. Before you rush off to buy anything, I recommend piling your dishes first and then deciding if you really need something. Many of my clients find that once they have finished choosing the dishes they love, removing dishes from the bottom of the pile no longer bothers them, and there's no need to buy storage goods.

To sum up, make the dishes you love the ones you use every day. Unpack them and stack them in your cupboard. This is guaranteed to bring you one step closer to a joyful dining table.

## Cutlery

Although people often ask me how to store their dishes, they rarely ask about how to store cutlery. Apparently, the fact that cutlery is the king of kitchen *komono* isn't widely known. I urge you to reserve the best space for your cutlery right from the start. Next to food and your toothbrush, cutlery is the only other thing that enters your mouth. Despite the delicate nature of its job, it works much longer hours than a toothbrush, and while working, it moves from the plate to your mouth and back again countless times, which must make it quite dizzy. By treating anything that directly touches your body with extra respect, you can multiply the joy factor in your daily life.

There are two ways of storing cutlery: by placing it upright in tubes or by laying it flat in a box. If you have no drawers in the kitchen and space conservation is your top priority, the best solution is to store your cutlery upright. The most common method is to place it in a leftover cup, which can then be stored in the dish cupboard.

The best storage method is to place knives, forks, spoons, and chopsticks in their own compartments within a cutlery tray or a box that is just the right size. If you are going to choose a cutlery tray, your cutlery will be happier if you pick one that is made of rattan, bamboo, or some other natural material with a gentle embrace, rather than a plastic case in which it will rattle around. By the way, my criterion for deciding which items require royal treatment (other than for such things as wallets and purses) is this: the item's proximity to your body. Items such as forks or undergarments, which come in direct contact with delicate parts of our bodies, should be treated as a rank above the rest whenever possible.

Once they start storing their cutlery like royalty, many of my clients want to use cutlery and chopstick rests at the table. Soon, they are looking for beautiful table mats and coasters, too. The thought of all that essence of joy being added to their dining table fills me with eager anticipation.

## *Komono* that brighten up your table

When I was working with one of my clients, a wooden napkin ring rolled out of her accessory box. When I told her what it was, she burst out laughing. 'I always wondered! It was too big for a ring and too small for a bangle.' What a tragedy for the forgotten napkin ring.

Place mats, tea mats, coasters and chopstick holders – they may not be essential, but they greatly enrich mealtime. If you have some, don't waste them. Use them every day.

The standard storage place for this *komono* category is near your dishes or cutlery, but anywhere near the kitchen or the dining table will do. If you have prettily designed napkin rings or chopstick rests, store them attractively. Why not line them up in your drawer like a beautiful store display so that every time you open it, they give you a thrill?

Kitchen *komono* made of cloth include two types: tools such as tea towels and 'accessories' such as place mats. For the first category, the basic approach is to fold and store them upright. The second category can be folded, rolled, or stacked, depending on the nature of the item. For people with minimal storage space in the kitchen, such as in studio apartments, it works well to store these in the wardrobe near where you keep other cloth *komono*.

## Cooking utensils

Ladles and spatulas are very tough. It's their job to leap bravely into the fray, sautéing meat or dishing up soup, while sparks fly between food and frying pan. Whereas cutlery and dishes nestle together in sets, cooking utensils usually work solo, one to each house, and they tend to be confident and assertive. For this reason, after your joy check, you don't need to take as much care when you store them.

The two basic approaches are to store them upright or lying down. Hanging them from hooks on the wall is another option, but avoid hanging kitchen scissors or other bladed tools because if they are hanging right in front of you, the possibility of being sliced will make you nervous even if you aren't aware of it. I also make it a rule to hang cooking utensils only where they won't be splattered with oil, which may be why, so far, none of my clients has hung any of them.

When storing upright, my standard approach is to put things in a utensil holder, a jug, or any other container that is sufficiently tall that it won't fall over and to place this in the cupboard. The most common approach, however, is to store them in drawers. Unlike cutlery, there's no need to divide them by category, so most utensils can be stored either directly in the drawer or in the lid of a box inside the drawer. Can openers, measuring spoons, and other small items, however, fare better if they are stored with a divider that separates them from larger utensils. If you have some spares that are still in their packages, you could get rid of your old ones and start using these.

## Cooking vessels

Take out all your cooking vessels and spread them on the floor or tabletop. This includes everything from metal and earthenware pots and frying pans to mixing bowls and colanders. Follow the basics of picking each one up and checking for joy.

When storing, stack similarly shaped items inside each other, such as pots with pots and bowls with bowls, so that you make the most of the cupboard's height. If your cupboards come with a built-in frying pan rack, use it.

## Cooking appliances

Gather all your cooking appliances, such as toasters, coffee machines and blenders, in one spot. Don't forget to gather those you keep in places other than the kitchen! Do you have any that you bought when they were a fad and have now tired of, or ones that you haven't used for years? My clients' kitchens have made known to me the incredible volume and diversity of cooking equipment and household appliances that exist in this world. This includes poached egg pans, deep fat fryers, juicers, apple peelers, shaved ice machines, nutcrackers and even flumes for serving chilled noodles in running water.

I currently use a mixer to make a green smoothie every morning, but even things like this that are used every day should be stored on a shelf or in a cupboard. It may seem a bit of a bother, but once you have decided where things belong, it really isn't much trouble. Please give it a try. My standard approach is to store seldom-used items in the back of the cupboard or on the top shelf, because it won't matter if they require a bit of effort to remove.

## Food storage containers

Food storage containers come in all kinds of materials and shapes, and include commercial containers made of plastic, glass and metal as well as empty jam jars and tea tins. While it is important to do your basic joy check, you should also check how many you have. Count all of them, including those currently in use in the fridge, and think objectively about how many you actually need. If you have more than you need, go ahead and discard any old ones. It's a good idea, however, to save some

square containers to use later as dividers in your kitchen drawers.

As for storing empty containers, you can significantly improve the efficiency of your storage space by stacking those that are stackable and storing their lids upright in a separate container. Alternatively, if you have extra space and are worried about dust getting into the containers, you can store them on the shelf with the lids on.

## Baking supplies

When I was still in primary school before I developed my passion for tidying, I loved baking and often spent my spare time making sweets. I still get a thrill when I see cake pans and cookie cutters shaped like hearts or animals, and I feel an urge to buy them even though I don't bake any more. But that's only when I see them in the store. When I see these things in my clients' homes, more often than not it's their desperate plea for help that stirs my heart, not joy. If you have any cake pans or cookie cutters that you bought but have almost never used and now lie rusting in a cupboard, get rid of them.

I don't know why, but the most common storage method for baking equipment seems to be to put everything in a plastic bag, tie it shut and throw it on a shelf. This is, of course, a no-no. Once in the bag, they seem to fade out of existence, perhaps because it's so hard to breathe in plastic. Or maybe it's because we naturally avert our gaze when it lands on such an unsightly lump on the shelf. Whatever the reason, the frequency with which people bake drops when baking things are stored this way.

Unlike cooking, baking sweets is something we do when we feel like it. Thus, baking goods are not really cooking utensils but hobby equipment. Baking equipment should spark joy, which is why wrapping them in a plastic bag is definitely out. If you don't use them that frequently and want to protect them from dust, at least store them in a soft bag made of cloth or more pliable plastic, not in a noisy shopping bag with the name of a supermarket emblazoned on it.

If you don't need to store them in a bag, stack cake tins and other large items just like dishes and put them directly on the shelf. Alternatively, you could store them in a box just for baking goods and place that on the shelf where you can see them. This is your chance to use that pretty box that you chose to keep.

## Disposables

The category that generally gets less use than any other is disposable kitchen *komono*, such as disposable chopsticks, straws, paper plates, cups and napkins. These are usually used as a set, and therefore it's fine to store them in a single box with everything standing upright. One of my clients said to me, 'I can't be bothered washing dishes, so I always use paper plates and cups.'

I asked her rather pointedly, 'Does that really and truly bring you joy?'

If you are tempted to use paper dishes for the same reason, then I urge you to store your disposable dishes at the very back of the topmost shelf to make them hard to get. Or you could even just dispose of them all right now! Whatever you choose, please remember that the purpose of tidying is to impart joy to every day of your life.

Because such items are often 'free', we end up accumulating too many before we realize it. Whether disposable chopsticks or spoons that come with a cup of ice cream, decide how many you really need and make up your mind to chuck the rest. If you don't need it, be sure to say so when a store clerk offers it.

## Plastic bags

Plastic and paper supermarket bags are one of the most common things people accumulate without thinking. I have tried many different ways of storing them. In my family, we used to store them in another plastic bag that was attached to the handle of a cupboard with a clothespin. This was anything but attractive, and certainly did not inspire joy. Worse, in our small kitchen, every time someone passed it, they would bump into it with a most annoying sound. Most of my clients use the same type of method, the only variation being to use a reusable nylon bag to hold them. Many people also tie their plastic bags in a knot. This is the worst approach because it just increases bulk. It also makes more work as you have to untie them when you want to use them.

There are storage items specifically designed for stocking plastic shopping bags, usually a cloth sleeve with a wide end at the top for inserting the bags and a narrow end at the bottom for extracting them one at a time, like tissue from a tissue box. There is nothing wrong with these, but to me they seem to take up more space than is necessary, and often when you pull out one bag, another is dragged out with it and falls to the floor like a lonely caterpillar. Besides, it goes against the grain to buy something especially to store disposable plastic bags.

One of my clients used the same method of storing plastic bags within another plastic bag. Although she insisted that her family of five needed a lot of bags to hold their rubbish, it was clear that she had far more than necessary. She told me she had been collecting bags for over thirty years. When I examined the outer bag that held the rest, I noticed that the bottom had yellowed. Dreading what I might find, I shoved my hand inside, grabbed the bag on the very bottom, and pulled it out. The instant it left the bag a puff of yellow powder showered through the air like roasted bonito flakes. It smelled far from fragrant, however. Whether it was disintegrated plastic or dust, I will never know, but the sour-smelling yellow flakes scattered across the floor. We counted a total of

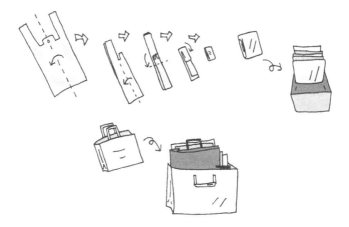

241 bags. Even if she used four bags a day, it would take her more than two months to use them all up.

The most common problems with plastic bag storage are storing too many and wasting space. We store too many because we don't have a clear idea of how many we actually have, and plastic bags waste space because they tend to inflate. If you aren't sure how many bags is too few or too many, you could try calculating how many you have used over the last three months. Items that tend to add up before we realize it are precisely the ones we should count.

When storing bags, pay attention to reducing bulk and store them in something rigid. Plastic bags should be flattened, folded, and stored upright just like clothes to prevent overstocking. If you can't be bothered folding plastic bags, store them in a compact box that keeps them from expanding. The container should be kept small, about half the size of a tissue box. This is large enough to fit up to twenty bags, whereas a shoebox, for example, fits about two hundred bags, resulting in serious oversupply. While paper bags can be stored in another paper bag, a file box, which is stiffer, will prevent you from accumulating more than you need.

## Small kitchen *komono*

This is the time to tidy up all those little kitchen *komono* that you haven't tackled yet, such as tablespoons and teaspoons, toothpicks and skewers, can openers and corkscrews. Discard any items that you have two or more of and those that you rarely use because you have a multipurpose tool that serves the purpose. Feel free, however, to hang on to those things that bring you joy regardless, such as a beautifully designed bottle opener.

The key to storing these items is to divide them thoroughly and store them in a drawer. Look for empty boxes or containers that are the perfect size to use as dividers.

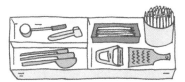

## Kitchen consumables

Consumables such as cling film, aluminium foil, parchment paper and paper towels can be stored in the cupboard or pantry, upright under the sink, or on racks that fasten to the door of your cupboard or the wall. If you have multiple boxes of things like zippered storage bags, remove them from their boxes and transfer them all to one container to save space. It is best to store consumables out of sight to enhance the joy factor. If you have too many supplies to fit in the kitchen, make a 'surplus supplies' *komono* category and store it somewhere else, such as in a cupboard or storage room.

If shelf liners, kitchen fan filters and anti-splatter panels to protect your walls from grease stains do not spark joy, one solution may be to remove them altogether. This is also a good time to reconsider those convenient-looking goods that are not actually very convenient.

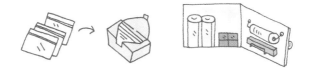

## Kitchen cleaning equipment

Kitchen cleaning equipment, such as detergent, sponges and cleansers, are generally stored together in a basket that is either placed in the cupboard under the sink or attached to the inside of the cupboard door. Basically, nothing should be kept near the sink, not even your dish detergent or sponge.

When I tell my clients this, they are often shocked. 'You mean you put your sponge away in the cupboard when it's wet?' they usually ask. The answer is no. Please dry it before putting it away. The trick is to squeeze the water out completely. If you squeeze it thoroughly with the intention of drying it, you will be surprised at how quickly it dries. Stand it up someplace where it will not be splashed with water, or hang it and then put it away as soon as it is dry. The point is to avoid keeping sponges around the sink. If you use yours so frequently that it never has a chance to dry completely, don't bother storing it in the cupboard, but do put away the detergent each time you use it. It's important to avoid keeping anything around the sink or on the counter that can cause water stains.

## No need to aim for simplicity in the kitchen

Having read this far, please don't assume that you must reduce a whole lot more to achieve joy. **It may seem like a contradiction, but you don't need to aim for simplicity in the kitchen.**

Walking through the kitchenware section in a store gives me an indescribable thrill of pleasure. Even though cooking is not my particular forte, I can spend hours staring at the rows of merchandise. There is so much variety in design, even for standard pots and pans, not to mention all the interesting gadgets, such as avocado slicers and gloves that let you peel burdock swiftly and easily.

After hearing a client rave about the benefits of some handy new gadget while giving a demonstration worthy of a TV shopping channel, I've been known to purchase one for myself on the way home. On the other hand, I have noticed that top sales items frequently vanish from my clients' homes after a certain period of time. When I ask why, the response is usually that it was hard to use, it broke or they got tired of it. Kitchen gadgets are similar to children's toys. They are fun to try when they catch our interest, but inevitably there will come a day when they no longer bring us joy. Although it would be ideal if we could continue using everything with care and respect, if an item has completed its role in our life, then it's time to thank it and bid it farewell.

The kitchen is the one place in the home where even when we have weeded out and discarded those things that no longer serve their purpose, there still seems to be a lot left. This frequently puzzles my clients. 'I'm almost finished tidying the kitchen, but I feel like there's still so much here,' they tell me. Perhaps they're imagining a kitchen like the ones they've seen in department stores or magazines in which all the equipment is neatly arranged in spacious cupboards. But when you consider the volume of things in a kitchen compared to the actual space available for storage, achieving that effect is no easy feat.

Due to the nature of my work, I have had many opportunities to observe the way people store things in other countries, and I would have to say that I have yet to come across a country where the kitchens give me as much of a thrill as those in Japan. Japanese kitchens just have such a wealth of diversity. Take spices and seasonings, for example. As a matter of course, Japanese homes stock them for Japanese, Chinese and Western cuisines, plus they often have spices to make exotic ethnic foods from around the world. Equipment also covers a broad range, from food processors to basket steamers. The shelves of Japanese dish cupboards display an array of dishes for every season and food, including nested boxes for special New Year's foods, glass bowls for chilled noodles and china sets with different patterns denoting each season.

A well-known food expert once remarked, 'The number of recipes created in Japan far exceeds the number produced in any other country.' I think it's no exaggeration to say that Japanese food culture is outstanding for its rich variety. Flavours, presentation, dishes, cooking equipment – all are characterized by beauty and diversity. These features of Japanese cuisine, which spring from the Japanese delight in the changing seasons and their pursuit of subtle differences, are a precious treasure that I feel we must pass on to the next generation.

But I digress. The point I wish to make is that when it comes to the kitchen, no matter which country you live in, there's no need to pursue simplicity to extremes. **What matters is the ability to see where everything is stored.** If you have achieved this, then even if storage space seems a bit full, you can still be proud of your kitchen. What I hope you will aim for is a kitchen where you feel happy just cooking, one that expresses your own unique brand of joy.

## Food

When tidying foodstuffs in the kitchen, I recommend leaving anything in the fridge until the very end. The first thing to check is the expiration date. Dried foods in particular can have a surprisingly short shelf life, something many of my clients are shocked to realize. The basic

rule is to discard anything that is past the expiration date, but if you have your own rules, such as 'two months over is okay for tinned goods', go ahead and use that as your criteria. When in doubt, ask yourself whether it would spark joy to cook something with it.

Do you have supplement drinks that you bought on a whim but never finished or health foods that you order merely from habit? This is an opportunity to reflect on whether your body really needs them or whether they are having an effect.

If you have bought or received so much of a certain item that you cannot possibly consume it all, ask your friends if they need some or donate the surplus to a food bank.

## STORING FOOD

Store food by category. Stand anything that can be stored upright. When you open the drawer or gaze upon your pantry shelf, you should be able to tell at a glance where everything is. The basic categories are seasonings, dried foods, dry carbohydrates (rice, pasta, etc.), tinned food, boil-in-the-bag foods, sweets, bread and supplements. If appearance matters to you, you can increase the joy factor significantly by transferring dried goods and other foods to matching canisters.

I recommend storing things together. For example, if you don't use small packages of seasonings that often, try emptying them into jars, one for each seasoning. It just takes little ideas like this to make your food storage more effective.

## USING LEFTOVER INGREDIENTS

If you discover a large stock of things that are near their expiration dates, use them all up at once. Have a 'borderline stock clearance campaign'. It can be fun to experiment with new recipes.

One of my clients who had just discovered a large stash of expired food startled me by announcing, 'Perfect! My boyfriend is coming tomorrow. I'll feed them to him!' Of course, she wasn't trying to be mean. She confidently assured me that expired food is often quite edible, and when I asked her later, she reported that everything worked out fine. I do, however, recommend that you use good judgement, including your sense of smell, and be prepared to accept the consequences.

## DRINKS

Drinks can be divided into two types: those that can be drunk as is (bottled and canned drinks, juice boxes, etc.) and dried or powdered drinks (tea, drink powders, etc.). First, check the expiration date. The first category in particular has a short shelf life because it contains liquid. Discard any that are out of date. Some that fall into the second category, such as green and breakfast tea, can be used even after they expire in incense lamps or as chips for smoking bacon and so on. Search for ways to make use of these items rather than discarding them if you can.

### PERISHABLES

Start by taking a quick look through your fridge and throwing out any items that have passed the expiration date. The fridge, by the way, is the one exception to the rule of removing every item to check it. If you have any individual sauce or seasoning packs or other things that you never use, throw them out. Store those you keep in a small box or storage container to make your fridge neater.

When storing things in the fridge, you want to keep it about 30 per cent empty. You can use the extra space for leftovers from the evening meal or any food you might receive that day. Store things by category so that it is clear at a glance where things are.

## Tricks for kitchen storage

When considering kitchen storage, think about the kitchen as a whole. Kitchen storage generally includes cupboards above and below the counter and sink, drawers and freestanding dish cabinets. Whereas a dish cabinet is designed with shelves and drawers specifically to store dishes, the areas under the sink and counters are often large empty spaces. As noted earlier, we should start storing by filling the large built-in spaces first.

As long as you divide your storage by category, you can store things wherever you like, but for the sake of those who want to be a little more particular, let me share some of my own thoughts on kitchen storage. When I visit homes for lessons, it's my practice to crawl into the cupboards and storage spaces once they have been emptied, or to at least stick my head in and test the air if I can't actually fit inside. The cupboard under the sink feels moist and humid, while the cupboards by the stove have a dry, crackling feel redolent of oil and flame. For this reason, I believe it's better to avoid storing items that are vulnerable to moisture under the sink. I was interested to learn yet again that feng shui supports my intuition. According to this philosophy, the element for the space under the kitchen sink is water while that for the space by the stove is fire.

The key to storage in cabinets is utilizing the height of these spaces. In some newer houses, these cupboards come with wire racks, but if yours don't, use things that have been freed up during the tidying process. Or if you just love storage goods, you're welcome to buy new ones. If you have a lot to store, it's less confusing to divide your things simply into 'frequent use' and 'infrequent use', rather than trying to categorize frequency of use by incremental degrees. Standard storage for things you use infrequently is to put them on the top shelves of a cupboard above the counter.

Feel free to make your own personal categories like 'bread-making equipment,' or 'cake-decorating supplies'. Start with the big items first when deciding where to store things. If you have a dish cabinet, store the dishes in it first, followed by cooking tools, seasonings, and so on.

When creating storage in your kitchen drawers, one way to ensure success is to constantly consider ways to reduce bulk. Take rubber bands, for example. Many people leave them in the box they came in and put this directly into a drawer, but this is a waste of space. As the bands are used, the box becomes increasingly empty, yet it still takes up the same amount of room in the drawer. You can save space by transferring the rubber bands to a small jar or other container. This will also make the inside of your drawer look nicer. As the amount of space occupied by your things decreases, you can begin moving things left out on the counter and elsewhere into the cupboards and drawers. In the end, even the kettle, the rice cooker and the rubbish bin end up behind cupboard doors, and

your kitchen is completely free of clutter! You may think this is impossible, but I encourage you to make this your goal as you store your things.

Tidying is a special event. If you give storage your best effort, experimenting with different ideas and enjoying the whole process, you'll find that it goes very smoothly. Treat it like a game. Each idea you try will bring immediate results, and you can readjust anytime you like. Storage is really the most entertaining attraction in the tidying carnival.

## Decorating your kitchen

Once you've tidied up your kitchen, take some time to make it look pretty. You can decorate it with wall art, put beautiful cloth that you love behind the glass in your dish cabinet, and attach tiles with pretty patterns to the wall. Decorating the kitchen can dramatically increase the joy effect, especially if you've never given a thought to making your kitchen look pretty before. I've mentioned in chapter 2 how one of my clients hung a corkboard in her kitchen and made a display corner for cards from her children and seasonal decorations. She found that this greatly increased her enjoyment of cooking.

I recommend gradually replacing the tools in your kitchen with things that spark joy. In my case, for example, I replaced a plastic spatula I was using without much thought for a wooden one, and this really opened my eyes to the difference it can make to use kitchen goods that spark joy. If you have even one daily kitchen item that you have chosen with great care, the time you spend cooking will be much more joyful.

## Making mealtime spark joy

When you have finished tidying, the next important step towards achieving your ideal kitchen is making mealtime joyful. Do you plan your menu and table settings to reflect the changing seasons? You can reflect the seasons very easily by using smaller items, such as place mats and chopstick rests. I pay particular attention to the latter. I have nineteen sets, including ones I made myself, and I not only match them to the season and to the ingredients I'm using, but I also use them to brighten up the dinner table when it needs more colour by placing a few around the table settings as accents. You can also try adding candles to your table.

Recently, 'daikon art', in which grated daikon is moulded into crazy animal shapes, has become a popular fad in Japan. It seems that many people are quite creative at adding a playful spirit to their meals. Please experiment and find what infuses your mealtimes with joy.

# Cleaning supplies

Any surplus house cleaning supplies or cleansers that you don't use can be donated to someplace that needs them. To select those that spark joy, imagine yourself using them for cleaning. Store the ones you choose to keep all together in a storage room or cupboard. Cleaning rags, or old towels that you plan to use for rags, should be stored folded and upright.

The cleanliness of your house is not necessarily proportional to the volume of your cleaning goods. Cleaning supplies are only of value if they are used. If you have any in your cupboard that have not even been opened, open them up and use them completely to do a thorough cleaning of all the storage spaces in your home.

# Laundry supplies

Items related to laundry should be stored near the washing machine. Personally, I like to take off the garish labels from my liquid laundry soap and tie a ribbon around the neck to increase the joy factor.

# Bathroom *komono*

Although it's hard for me to admit, I never once succeeded in tidying the space under the sink in my
parents' home when I lived there. I never did understand why, but there was always far too much stuff – extra
toothbrushes, makeup samples, body soaps. Yet that did
not give me the right to throw any of it away. Worse still,
the area around the sink was always damp. I tried nagging
people to wipe up after themselves, but this only made
everyone grumpy, so that even I lost the courage to insist.
My response was to clean up silently.

By that time, I had come a long way. Having been
banned from tidying after secretly disposing of my family's belongings, I had learned the hard way that meddling
with other people's things isn't worth it in the end. The
only solution, I decided, was to make the space as pleas-
ant as possible at least when I was using it. Cleaning the
bathroom sink without complaint would be my way of
thanking my parents for letting me live in their house.
Not only did I clean it every time I used it, but I also
gave it a wipe whenever I passed by. Once a month, I
took the things off the glass shelves beside the sink and
wiped the shelves thoroughly. I was quite faithful about
keeping it clean, yet if I couldn't get to it due to work or
if I forgot even once, the area quickly became damp and
slimy, which was very discouraging.

The bathroom, which often gets very little attention

when we're tidying, can actually be one of the hardest places to keep tidy. It gets wet, houses a huge volume of extra supplies and often has multiple users.

When considering storage for each place, I always think about the purpose it serves. The bathroom is used for washing one's face, brushing one's teeth and bathing. In Japan, it may also be where the washing machine is located and where people do their laundry. I think of it as the place for storing water- and skin-related things, the main categories of which are as follows:

Face and body cleansing items (consumables such as skin and hair care products, toothbrushes, hair dryers, hairbands, hairpins, cotton pads, razors, as well as extra supplies of the same and towels)

Bath-related items (shampoo, bath salts, etc.)

Cleansing items (bath cleanser, sponges, etc.)

The tidying campaign is your chance to review, item by item, your supplies of tissue, shampoo and so on. Any items that are so old that their quality is suspect, or that you simply do not use any more, should be dealt with now.

While the ideal is to use them up, if you have too many, you can donate them. The key point in managing supplies is to know your figures. Estimate how many days it would take to use up one item and then calculate how many days' worth of those items you have on hand. If you have not just one year's supply, but five or six, you can turn this into material for comic relief. Take photos to show your friends, spin it into a heroic tale of your tidying marathon and have fun while you carry on with tidying.

If your sink stand has drawers, you can simply apply the two basic principles: store by category and store upright. The cupboard under the sink, however, requires special attention. When people tell me they are having trouble with bathroom storage, it's usually because they are not uti-lizing the space under the sink effectively. When I open the cupboard door, I'll find cleansers and shampoos all jammed together on the floor with a gaping void above them.

To make the best use of the space under the sink where there is no shelf, utilize its height. This is one case where boxes are not enough, and storage goods come to the rescue. I often use a set of smallish plastic drawers left over from tidying *komono*. If the set of drawers is deep enough, it can be inserted under the sink as is. If there is still room above it, put a lidless box on top so that you can store taller items such as bottles and your hair dryer in it, exploiting the cupboard's height.

If the set of drawers is the right depth but too tall for the cupboard, my standard procedure is to take it apart where possible. To do this, remove all the drawers and turn the frame upside down, then slide out the parts. You can fit these back together to make a shorter case with fewer drawers. Casters are also removable.

A simple rack with legs also works well instead of plastic drawers. If you don't have either, place a lidless

box on top of a plastic storage box. This will make it hard to open the storage box so it's best to use it to store only extra supplies of consumables, such as toothbrushes and soap. That way you can minimize the number of times you need to open it.

If you share a bathroom with others, start by storing communal items first before moving on to personal items. Items with high communal use include toothbrush holders, toothpaste, hair dryers, towels and cleansers. Once you've finished making room for these items, you can divide the remaining space among the individuals who live there so that each person has his or her own place to store personal skincare products and so on.

If there isn't enough space in the bathroom, have each person store personal items in his or her own room. How you go about this will depend on your family, but I recommend setting clear ground rules. When making them, don't forget to include a strategy to keep the sink area dry. I solved this problem in my own house by copying what one of my clients did, and now my sink is always sparkling. She simply kept a towel in the washroom specifically for wiping the sink. You may be surprised that I had never thought of this, but I often gain practical tips like these from my clients.

As I'm sure you've noticed, I'm always encouraging people to store things upright, from clothes to stationery goods to makeup. So people often ask me, 'Should I store my towels upright, too? Can't I pile them?' They may be recalling how nice the towels in hotels look when piled and even colour coordinated. There are two reasons why I recommend storing things upright. One is because it makes things much easier. You can see at a glance what is there, quickly pick out what you need, and extract or return an item without disturbing the rest. The other reason is because the things at the bottom of a pile become squished and look miserable.

Towels, however, are usually used in order from top to bottom. We don't usually go to the trouble of selecting a specific towel from somewhere in the pile. As long as you make sure to place newly washed towels on the bottom and always use the towel on the top, the pile will stay neat and tidy. Towels are often used quite frequently, and therefore the one on the bottom will only be there for a short time. So, yes, it really is okay to pile your towels. But if you prefer to select which towel you use, then it's also fine to fold and roll them like clothes and stand them up in a basket on the shelf.

## Transform your bathroom into a joyful space

The scenery reflected in the bathroom mirror is also very important. Mirrors tend to multiply the energy of whatever they reflect, so strive to make the background reflected in it as beautiful as you can. If it reflects a messy storage area, hang a cover over the storage unit or store your things in matching boxes to make them neat.

I also recommend hanging a beautiful picture on the wall reflected by the mirror. This will keep you spellbound by joy. Just make sure the frame is resistant to humidity.

## Pay particular attention to appearance when storing toilet-related articles

A high percentage of my clients tell me that they have no trouble storing toilet-related items, which are limited in number: just toilet paper, cleansers, deodorizers and feminine hygiene products. As long as you don't keep an excessive amount of extras on hand, storage is comparatively easy, and most of my clients make few errors in this department. Yet perhaps that's why I rarely run into a client with a perfect score. To be honest, it's also one area where I, too, used to be rather careless. A visit from a friend, however, changed everything.

'You were out of toilet paper, so I took out a new one,' she told me casually after using the toilet. I froze. To my chagrin, I realized that I had failed to take storing toilet paper seriously.

Don't tell me she opened that cupboard, I thought. How could she do that without asking? But then I realized that it was my own fault for not making sure there was an extra roll ready for use. After all, she couldn't very well have left the bathroom without it, could she?

Once she had gone home, I opened the cupboard door. The usual items were there in plain sight. They didn't look cluttered but their packages loudly proclaimed their contents, and it was anything but a joyful storage space, even though I make my living at tidying up – even though I'm always telling my clients they should pay particular attention to making hidden spaces joyful!

When I thought about it carefully, I realized that the bathroom – or the guest bathroom, if you have more than one – is the most public space in a person's home, even more public than the kitchen. Yet toilet-related items are the least thrilling items in the house. While visitors may rarely see them, if they look messy, you're out. Thus, toilet-related storage is where appearance matters most.

If your bathroom has a built-in cupboard, storage is simple. The rule of thumb is to store everything inside it in such a way that you won't feel embarrassed if someone else happens to open it. The same is true if you have a shelf above the toilet. Toilet paper is best stored in a basket or box. If you can't find one that works for you, you can leave the rolls in the package and place them directly on the shelf. If you have only one or two left and the package is floppy, it will look neater if you get rid of the package and leave them unwrapped on the shelf. If you have too much stock to fit on the shelf, store the remainder with your extra supplies of consumables.

As for deodorizing sprays and cleansers, remove any garish seals from their tops. You can even remove the labelling entirely from things you use frequently, such as the toilet cleanser or toilet wipes. Packages for toilet-related products tend to be loud and ugly, and removing them goes a long way to making the inside of the cupboard look more refined. Don't remove the packaging seals if you have children in the house, however, or for infrequently used products, such as drain cleansers, as you may need the seals to identify the contents.

Last but not least are feminine hygiene products. Storing them in the plastic bags from the drugstore is out of the question. The best solution is to store them in a rattan basket or a box that brings you joy. Any extra can be stored in a cloth bag you like. If you're living with your family and there's not enough room to store feminine hygiene products near the toilet, make a separate space in your wardrobe or elsewhere for them.

Your toilet storage is now complete. That wasn't so much trouble, was it? It only takes ten minutes max once you find the right box or bag in which to store things.

If your bathroom has a separate water closet or toilet area, look at how to increase the joy factor. It would be a shame to stop at merely storing your stuff randomly when you can completely transform this space with just a minimum of decoration. Start by looking at what's already there. Perhaps it's a calendar that you have hung there every year for no particular reason. Or is there a pile of books or magazines that you never read? Do any of these things spark joy?

The toilet is for discharging; it's a space devoted 100 per cent to output. Therefore, I feel that textual input should be avoided unless it's something you find truly inspiring. Instead, use things that appeal to the senses, such as aroma oils, flowers, a picture or ornament. Choose a toilet cover and mat that you particularly like. Impart your own personal touch.

Have you ever visited the bathroom in a restaurant or public place and been delighted to find the design concept fits the venue perfectly? In a Hawaiian café, for example, the door might be decorated with hibiscus and plumeria flowers, the walls with paintings of palm trees or hula dancers, and the washbasin with a tortoise ornament; and the air might be fragrant with the scent of coconut. Just stepping into the room can make you feel happy.

If you and your family have clearly defined tastes and ornaments you can use, it can be a lot of fun to turn your water closet into a joy-filled theme park like this. Especially if your toilet area is separate from the rest of the bathroom, because no one spends very long in it, it's safe to inject a pretty potent dose of joy. Of course, if you prefer tranquillity or like to keep things simple, you can adjust the amount accordingly.

If your toilet and bath are in the same room, then cleanliness must be given top priority, and you should strive to control mould and scaling. It will be much easier to maintain joy in this space if you keep everything closed and only use decorations made of suitably waterproof materials. It goes without saying that keeping the toilet clean is the key to maintaining a joyful space. Aim to have nothing on the floor except the toilet brush and a small wastebasket.

## ELIMINATE ESSENCE OF 'UN-JOY'

Almost as important as adding more joy is eliminating essence of 'un-joy'. By this, I mean things that spark no joy at all and are really just extraneous appendages. The thin transparent seal that covers the LCD of your audio equipment or the crinkly cellophane wrapper on the arrangement of dried flowers you received as a gift, for example, are really 'I-can-do-without-it' items.

The same goes for the words 'Power Pressure!' emblazoned on a rice cooker, the moving company logo stamped across the cardboard boxes in the cupboard, or the words 'Cotton Pads' in large print on the cotton pad carton. The more textual information you have in your environment, the more your home becomes filled with noise.

Just by eliminating these elements from your home, you can create an elegant space. The effects are immense. If you're aiming for the pinnacle of joy, I highly recommend it.

# 8

# Tidying sentimental items

## Tidying sentimental items means putting the past in order

At last, you have reached the final stage of your tidying campaign: sentimental items. The most important thing when tidying this category is to believe in your own sense of joy. You may wonder why I say this now, but let me remind you once again: by now your ability to discern joy is completely different than when you first started. If you have worked hard at storing things in the right order, from clothes to books to papers and to the voluminous *komono* category, you have sufficiently honed your sensitivity to what sparks joy that you can now relax and proceed with tidying your sentimental items.

There are a few important points to keep in mind. First, there is one thing you must never do: don't send sentimental items to your parents' home. There was a time when I thought it was all right for my clients to send things home as long as their parents had room. But when I helped those parents to tidy up their own home, I realized that they could not proceed because they had a huge stack of boxes from their children. Moreover, once sent home, those boxes were almost never opened.

Secondly, if you cannot bring yourself to throw something away, keep it with confidence. It might be a T-shirt designed by your high school class for a school festival, for example, but if you can't part with it, keep it. Don't berate yourself for not being able to throw away something as simple as that. Rather, trust your instincts, which you have already honed by choosing what to keep and what to discard for an astounding number of things. As long as you have approached that T-shirt with integrity, the day will come when you know that it has fulfilled its job.

Finally, make good use of the things you choose to keep for the next stage of your life. If you're going to go to all the trouble of choosing sentimental items that spark joy, then it's important to keep them in a way that lets you enjoy them whenever you want. 'Will the future me need this to spark joy?' Use this as your criterion to confront each item and put your past self in order.

# Putting school memories in order

Every student during his or her school life receives report cards and graduation certificates. If you want to keep your report cards as a keepsake, one method is to choose only the one that made the greatest impression on you. Personally, however, I thanked all of these things and then discarded them.

If you can't bring yourself to get rid of your school uniform, why don't you try wearing it and lose yourself in memories of your youth? Most of my clients who do this come to their senses and discard it.

# Putting memories of past lovers in order

You may have many mementos from a past love: gifts, matching clothes, photo-booth strips. If you hope to develop a relationship with someone new, the basic approach is to get rid of everything. The exception are things that you have used for so long on a daily basis that they no longer bring back any memories of that relationship.

Regardless of what memories you have, never take out your negative feelings on your things. Always thank them for the wonderful memories and part from them with gratitude.

If you feel the need to clean away any karma that might cling to photos of someone you've broken up with, throw in a pinch of purification salt, and hide the faces by placing them in an envelope or paper bag with the pictures facing inward so that you can't see them from the outside. This method of using a paper bag and purification salt works not only for photos and stuffed toys but also for anything to which you feel some sort of emotional tie, such as items belonging to someone who has passed away.

One of my clients who was discarding mementos of a former boyfriend threw salt in the bag so forcefully she seemed to be driving out demons. As she tied the bag shut, she remarked, 'I haven't felt this way since that day. Now I can get on with my life.' With a peaceful expression she had never shown before, she put her hands together and bowed to the bag, saying, 'Thank you for everything.' What happened on 'that day' I have no idea, but the salt appeared to have done its job.

## Sentimental recordings

Sentimental recordings include those of old TV shows as well as of different events in your life. Videos without labels can be a real problem when doing the joy check. If you need to determine the content, limit yourself to watching only the very beginning and make your decision immediately. If you have a lot, set aside a time to do it and do it quickly, all in one go. Personally, I am totally in favour of discarding them all without checking the contents. If you can transfer the data from the videos you choose to keep to DVDs or a hard drive, you can save a great deal of physical storage space.

## Your children's creations

There are various ways of approaching this category, such as taking photos of your children's art before throwing it away or deciding how many you will keep and sticking to that number. If, however, there are items that you cannot bring yourself to part with now, there is no need to force yourself to discard them. If you are going to keep them, however, it is important to take care of them. I recommend designating a specific corner for displaying these works. Once you have enjoyed the works to the full, you can thank them for helping your child to grow, and discard them guilt-free.

225

# Life records

If you decide to keep such mementos as ticket stubs from your travels, always save them in a way that they can be enjoyed at any time, such as by putting them in a scrapbook.

For datebooks, you could choose one from the most joyful year to keep. In the case of diaries, at this point you can flip through them and reminisce about things that happened, keeping only those that still spark joy. Or you can adopt the criterion of one of my clients, which was to discard those that she would have felt embarrassed to have anyone read after she died.

# Letters

Take another look at each letter you have received. Say goodbye with gratitude to those that have finished their purpose. Rather than putting them directly into the recycle bin, it is more respectful to cover them in a paper bag first.

Continue to treasure any letters that still encourage you or touch your heart when you read them again. As letters deteriorate over time, store them in a container that is ventilated and in a place with low humidity. If you like, choose a box that you really love to keep them in.

# Tidying your photos as the final step in your campaign

As usual, take each photo in your hands and keep only those that spark joy. The basic rule is to remove all photos from their albums, but you don't need to do this for any albums that spark joy as a whole.

Even if you have two cardboard boxes filled with photos, do not falter. With your current level of sensitivity, you will be amazed at how quickly you can select those that you wish to keep. Let go of any that are similar or that are of scenes you don't really remember. The basic approach to negatives is to discard them all. One of my clients declared that she would keep only those photos in which she looked good, which, in a sense, is actually the correct criterion.

During the selection process, it helps to lay all the photos on the floor according to year. This way you can enjoy organizing your past. Putting them in an album that you really like is the indispensable and final step of the joy check. Photos will only keep your memories alive when they have been arranged so that you can enjoy them whenever you like.

## Tidy family photos with your family

I have a confession to make. I only finished tidying up my photographs very recently. Of course, I long ago finished tidying up photos of my own and those taken after I entered university, but I had not been able to touch any photos taken with my family when I was little. Just the other day, however, my father told me that he had found a huge cache of old photos – five cardboard boxes full in the very back of the cabinet. I wondered what to do. Should I ask him to get started on them, or should I buckle down and tackle the job myself? In the end, I decided that we would do it together as a family.

The following week I went to my parents' house, pulled the photos out of the boxes, spread them on the floor, and started the last chapter of our tidying festival. Sorting through these photos as a family, laughing and talking about our memories as we decided which ones to keep, was probably the happiest tidying job I have ever done. And that gave me an idea. I decided to make a proper album of our memories as a gift for my parents. I had not made anything for my parents since I was in kindergarten, and, to be honest, I actually decided to do it as part of my research on the subject of tidying.

You see, I was curious. Although my parents had taken their share of photos of important family events, like birthdays and Christmas, I couldn't recall them ever stopping to look at those photos with us and reminisce about the past. In contrast, some of my clients proudly show me lovely albums filled with memories and appear to really enjoy spending time looking through them. I was curious to see if the fact that my parents didn't do this was a personality trait or simply because they had never tried it, and also to find out whether making an album would have an impact on the way they tidied. As you can see, my motives were highly suspect, exposing me for the tidying freak that I am.

It just so happened that my mother's birthday was only two weeks away. I made a date with my younger sister to make an album that traced my parents' lives after they got married. The first step was to find an album that sparked joy. I picked one with an elegant gold pattern on a rose pink background. It was just the right size, neither too big nor too small, so that it would be easy for my parents to look at it again and again. It fit two photos to a page for a total of one hundred photos.

Now that we knew how many photos we needed, it was time to choose them. We divided up the enormous stash and looked at them one by one. Our criteria were simple: my mother must look pretty; some of the family must be with her; and, of course, the photos must spark joy. My sister was overwhelmed by the sheer volume at first, but we worked away steadily and within a little under two hours had narrowed it down to one hundred.

But we weren't finished yet. Photos these days are — you guessed it — digital! Since the advent of the digital camera, people take endless photos but rarely look at them more than once. My sister and I divided up the memory cards, of which there were about twenty, and began selecting only the very best shots. **When tidying up digital data, the same principle applies: choose what you wish to keep, not what you are going to discard.** You will never finish if you approach it by trying to decide which ones to erase when there are so many possibilities.

Start by making a new folder in your computer (I called mine 'joy photos') and move all the photos you choose into this folder. If you have photos from the same day, choose only the best one. With concentration, it only took us one hour to narrow our collection down to thirty photos. These we printed out.

This is where the real work begins. Lay all the photos on the floor according to the year in which they were taken, advancing from left to right until you reach the most recent. Photos from the same year should be lined up in a vertical row underneath. If you aren't sure when a photo was taken, make a guess.

'Dad's glasses look like they're from the eighties.'

'We went to Nagasaki when I was in elementary school, right?'

By the time you finish, your floor will look like you are playing multiple games of solitaire. This arrangement lets you see if there are more photos in some years than others or photos of similar situations. These can be weeded out until you have only your target number left. Now you can put them all into the album in one go, adding a few stickers and labels for decoration. The final product is pretty impressive.

By the time we had finished, I had totally forgotten that I was doing this for research and was purely focused on making something my mother would enjoy. The result was a huge success. My mother and father, who had never looked at their photos before, have since begun to print out their digital photos and look at them again. I now invite my clients to make an album for their parents as part of my lesson on tidying sentimental items. Or, if their parents have already passed away, I suggest making a memorial album, which allows them to look back over their parents' lives.

The comments I hear are quite varied.

'I haven't done something like this since I was in school, but it's really kind of fun!'

'I had always felt kind of distant from my parents, but when I look at each photograph, I think about how they really did love me and did their best to raise me – and I feel gratitude towards them.'

But in the end, all my clients, even those who are still in their twenties, agree that they should have tidied up their photos much earlier. I felt the same way. **It's never too late to start.** If you can, though, it's best to tackle your sentimental items as soon as possible once you're past the age of twenty-five so that you can put your life in order and fill your days with joy.

PART III

# Life-changing magic

# 9

# A home that sparks joy

## An entranceway that sparks joy

As a self-proclaimed tidying freak, I can tell the state of a person's wardrobes the instant I set foot in the doorway. One client's front entranceway was jammed with shoes and a bundle of newspapers ready for recycle. Keys, gloves, and delivery forms were strewn randomly across the top of the shoe storage bench, and the hallway was so packed with boxes of books and clothes that it looked like a storage shed. 'You'll have to come in the back door,' she said. 'There's no room to get in here.' Predictably, her home looked like a warehouse. While this is an extreme example, any home with a cluttered entranceway is bound to be cluttered throughout.

Even when the entranceway at first glance appears quite neat, if the air flow feels heavy, it's quite likely that the cupboards are stuffed to bursting. In fact, air circulation is an important consideration when tidying the entrance-way, and something I think about as I plan overall storage in a house. My cardinal rule is to observe how the air from the entranceway flows through the rest of the house and to make sure nothing obstructs it. If the entranceway is full of shoes and other things, the atmosphere in the home will be suffocating.

That's why I recommend keeping your entranceway as clear as possible. Leave out only the shoes you have worn that day to air them. This means that there will only be as many shoes as family members visible. Things that are needed during a certain period of your life, such as a baby carriage, can be stored here, too.

It's preferable to keep as little as possible in the entranceway. I suggest that you choose just one thing you really love to spark joy in this space. If you want to display several small things, you can prevent them from looking

like clutter by placing them on a tray or a cloth so that together they make a single decoration. Save the other things you love for decorating the rest of your house.

# A living room that sparks joy

The living room's role is to provide a space for the family to gather and enjoy each other's company. Always keep in mind that it's the centre of family life.

The ideal living room will feature furniture that sparks joy. I recommend having a fixed place for the remote control, magazines and so on. Consider adding plants, music you love and a special corner for family photos.

# A kitchen that sparks joy

Cleanliness is crucial. Moisture and oil are the enemy. That's why ease of cleaning gets top priority. Don't keep anything on the counter near the stove or sink. Keep pots and pans to a minimum, store all cooking utensils in one spot, and take advantage of vertical storage solutions for foodstuffs.

Decorate your kitchen, too. Your kitchen should make cooking fun.

# An office that sparks joy

You can clear your mind simply by discarding all unnecessary papers. Keep the desk area relatively clear. Arrange books and materials according to your own rules.

Consider adding a small ornamental plant. Don't make your office solely practical. It's important to add a playful touch precisely because it's a work space.

## A bedroom that sparks joy

Make your bedroom a space to recharge your batteries and refresh yourself for another day. Keep lighting soft and indirect, play relaxing music, and feature items and scents that spark joy. Wash sheets and pillowcases frequently.

# A bathroom that sparks joy

Why not enjoy your bathroom's delights? Bathe by candlelight and add bath salts, flowers, whatever you feel like.

Keep the tub and counters well scrubbed. Take out only what you need and put it away when finished.

The toilet is your home's 'detox area'. It's important to keep the energy flowing through, so keep it uncluttered. Any decorations should spark joy and be arranged with flow in mind. Cleanliness is crucial. The ideal water closet will have a fresh, natural aroma. Keep supplies like toilet paper out of sight in a basket or covered by a cloth.

# 10

# The changes that come when you're done

There was a period in my life when all I did was work. While I was grateful that people kept calling to ask for lessons, even when I saw two clients per day I couldn't keep up. Sometimes I gave three lessons a day, the first one from seven in the morning until noon, followed by a second one from one o'clock until five, and then finished off with another from six until eleven at night. Not only that, but when I came home, I had to write my book. I really love my job, but there were times when I would suddenly realize that I hadn't eaten for two days. I might as well have been living in the middle of the Sahara Desert, not metropolitan Tokyo. If I continued like this, I was afraid that I would end up in the hospital from too much tidying.

One evening, just when I was beginning to think that I was reaching the limit of what I could do on my own, my mobile phone buzzed. It was an email from a graduate of my classes named Mayumi.

'KonMari,' she wrote, 'would you take me on as your apprentice?'

What a surprise! Just the day before I had written up a list of graduates with the idea of asking them to help. Mayumi's name was at the very top. She had taken my lessons over half a year ago. I'm embarrassed to say that when I first met her, I thought that she was a bit hard to fathom. 'Tidying is on my to-do list every month, but my house never gets cleaned up . . . I feel like I'm tidying all the time,' she had said; but she was so timid that her voice faded away at the end of every phrase. She had gone to art school because she liked drawing as a child, but gave up on the idea of design right in the middle of job hunting and went to work in a variety shop 'because I like variety goods'. After a while, she was promoted to shop manager but decided to quit when she realized that she hadn't really wanted to be a manager. When I met her, she was working as a part-time salesperson, a job to which someone she knew had introduced her.

'I think I'm just no good at anything. I've never managed to finish what I set out to do. I wonder if I'm really capable of tidying . . . I can't see myself carrying on at this job forever, but I haven't a clue what I really want to do . . . I feel so unsure about everything.'

That was Mayumi. Yet by our second lesson, she was already beginning to change. 'Hi!' she said as she opened the door. She was wearing a black blazer over a crimson dress accented with ribbons. This was a marked contrast to the grey hoodie and jeans she had worn at our first lesson. I always wear a proper blazer when I work to show my respect to each person's home, but she was the first of my clients to dress up for a lesson. 'I decided that from now on I want to face my things properly,' she explained. I can still remember my amazement at her clear, confident tone.

It was this woman who became my apprentice, and her passion for tidying has been quite astonishing to see. Whenever she can, she accompanies me to my lessons as my assistant. She carries out the garbage bags, helps gather clothes and shreds confidential papers. When necessary, she will grab a hammer and dismantle a wire rack or assemble a cuckoo clock that has never been unpacked and hang it on the wall. While I'm talking with my clients, she sits unobtrusively on the floor, observing my lessons intently. After the day's lesson, we sit in a café drinking tea and going over the tricks of the tidying trade.

She always carries her little notebook in which she records in detail what I say, what she learns and all the secrets of storing. It's been two years since she became my apprentice and to me, she seems like a totally different person. Not only has she noticeably honed her tidying skills, but her words and behaviour are now filled with confidence. The other day I asked her casually, 'Mayumi, is your life joyful?'

'Yes!' was her emphatic reply.

To the people around her, the transformation may not seem so obvious, but even small changes will, in the end, totally transform a person's life. Without a doubt, tidying will change your life, too. By that, I don't mean that you'll suddenly become socially successful or immensely wealthy, although many people do as a result. The greatest change that occurs through tidying is that you will learn to like yourself.

When you tidy, you gain a little confidence.

You start to believe in the future.

Things begin to go more smoothly.

The people you meet change.

Unexpected things happen in a positive way.

Change begins to accelerate.

And you begin to really enjoy your life.

Not just Mayumi, but everyone can experience this. Once they taste the satisfaction that comes with tidying up, everyone, no matter who they are, wants to tell others about it, and they speak with passion about the transformation they've experienced. **Tidying is contagious.**

The sight of Mayumi, who once hated tidying, speaking about it so enthusiastically, always reminds me of the magic of tidying.

# Tidy up and put your love life in order

When I ask my Japanese clients 'What kind of room do you want?' for some reason many of them say, 'A room that will help me attract love and get married.' I am not an expert on how to increase your luck at love or marriage through tidying. However, I often hear from my clients that their love lives went more smoothly once they had tidied up. The reasons for this are varied. For some, overcoming an inferiority complex about tidying instilled confidence, making the person more proactive about love. For others, tidying up has increased the spark in their relationship so that they pop the question. I also receive reports that as a result of tidying, my clients have decided to terminate a relationship. **No matter the direction of the outcome, it is clear that tidying can also help us set our love life in order.**

When I interviewed N before her first lesson, our conversation shifted from tidying to her concerns about her love life. 'I'm not sure the guy I'm dating is the right person for me,' she confided. They had been going out for three years and worked at the same company. Some of his clothes and other belongings were in her apartment, but as it was not my job to advise her on her love life, I limited my advice to tidying. Yet from watching my clients, I have learned that when people are uncertain of their relationship, they tend to have a lot of unsorted documents. N was no exception. She had chequebooks that she never used, forms that she should have filled out to let various places know she had moved, recipe clippings that she had intended to file someday. And on and on.

'I guess I have other things I should be dealing with first, before I worry about my love life,' she laughed. I left her with the homework assignment of sorting all these papers before our next lesson. When I came back, she looked totally different, almost carefree. She had aced her homework and had taken a day off to fill out and send off all the forms. Not only that, as she tidied up, she had realized that she could no longer deny the ambiguity she felt about her relationship, and she and her boyfriend had decided to temporarily put a little distance between them.

'I wanted to give myself space to sort through my feelings,' she explained.

We finished in just two lessons. I did not see N again for about five months. The next time we had an opportunity to meet, I was surprised to learn that she and her boyfriend were getting married. 'After we had spent some time apart, he asked me to marry him. If I had still been feeling ambiguous, I might have hesitated. But during the time we had been apart, my feelings had become quite clear. I now had confidence in what made me happy, so I was able to say yes straight from my heart.'

I was touched by the happiness that shone in her eyes as she spoke.

Having served as a consultant for many years, I've learned that people who haven't yet met someone they really like tend to have accumulated a lot of old clothes and papers, while people who are in a relationship but are feeling ambiguous about it tend to be careless with their things. Our relationships with other people are reflected in our relationships with our things, and likewise our relationships with things show up in our relationships with people.

# Tidying brings relationships into focus

Close to half of my clients are parents who are raising children. During my lessons, I have seen just how hard it is to raise children while working, especially when those children are still very young.

One of my clients, F, lived with her husband and two children aged two and four. Both she and her husband worked as elementary school teachers. 'I'm always tired,' she confided. 'When I come home from work, I'm too exhausted to even pick up the rubbish from the floor. Then I feel guilty that I can't even do something as simple as that . . . My husband gets home late, but I hate to complain, because I know his work is really hard, too . . . I used to really love this job, but sometimes I lose confidence and wonder if it's okay to go on like this . . . My whole life right now is focused on "coping" and "getting through it" so I'd like to make some time when I can just relax and drink some tea from a favourite cup.'

By the time F finished tidying up, she knew that she really did love her job. She recognized that the textbooks, which she had thought were a nuisance and should be discarded, gave her joy. 'My closet was so full of secondary things that I couldn't take care of the things that really mattered. And I couldn't take care of myself either, really. I'm still too busy, and the laundry piles up before I know it. And there are still times when I'm so tired I don't feel like doing anything. But I'm not anxious any more. I can forgive myself for being tired and give myself a break.'

Her relationship with her husband changed, too. Up until then, each one had been working hard to fulfil his or her own separate role, but now they are consciously working together to build their family. She and her husband share their thoughts about the future and taking classes together. 'We each spent time thinking about the kind of life we wanted to live in twenty years. When we shared our vision, we found out that we both want to live in the same house that we live in now. For the first time in our marriage, I was able to tell him that I was glad I had married him, even though I felt a bit shy to say that.'

The changes tidying brought about in F's work and her relationships may not have been earth-shattering, but 'the number of times when I suddenly stop in the middle of cooking or folding laundry and realize that I'm happy has definitely increased'. This is a very common response from people who have finished tidying. I have learned from my clients that what really brings joy to our lives is savouring daily life, instead of taking it for granted.

# If your family's stuff bothers you, be like the sun

'How can I help my mother learn how to tidy up her stuff?'

'My wife needs your lessons.'

I often receive messages like these. As you move along with your own tidying process, your family's things and spaces can really start bothering you. 'My husband seems to have been inspired by my tidying up. He's reduced a few things, but nowhere near enough. There must be something I can do to make him take it more seriously.'

How well I know that feeling, the irritation that occurs when you see the stark gap between your own space and that of the rest of your family.

'I just can't stand the sight of my husband's stuff,' Y told me with a sigh. She lived with her husband and two children and had almost reached the end of her lessons. All that she had left was to finish tidying her kitchen things and storing things in the entranceway and bathroom. She had reduced a lot of her own stuff and was very pleased with her wardrobe and dresser that were now filled only with the things she loved. But her husband's space, which was half of an eight-tatami-mat (twelve by twelve-foot) room they had divided, had begun to bother her.

'From my perspective, it's just full of junk,' she said. The narrow area was filled with model tanks, figurines from Japan's warring states period and miniature castles. It was indeed a far cry from the simple, natural interior to which Y aspired, yet within it I could discern that her husband had a sense of order, and it was by no means messy.

'He uses the top half of the bookcase and I use the bottom, but every time I go to get a book, words like "warring states" leap out at me from his side, and I just can't stand it.'

She sounded quite biased, so I asked her, 'Has your husband ever talked to you about his interests?'

'Why would he? It's clear that I couldn't care less.'

I decided to give her a homework assignment. 'If you don't like something that belongs to someone else, the rule is not to look at or pay attention to it. But if you just can't help seeing your husband's things and they really bother you, then I want you to reach out and actually touch them. For example, you could pick up a figurine or run your finger lightly over the cover of a book. It doesn't matter how, but touch it and look at it carefully for at least a whole minute.'

When I came back for the next lesson, I asked her how it went. 'At first, I didn't even want to touch them, and quite frankly, I thought the assignment was going to be a pain. But strangely enough, when I gazed at an object for over a minute, I began to think in ways that had never occurred to me before. I would look at a miniature castle and find myself thinking, "Look at the tiny little parts it's made of," or touch a T-shirt with the name of a famous general on it and think, "I wonder what he feels like when he wears this." In the end, I actually felt grateful to these things for bringing joy into my husband's life.' Her homework had been a huge success.

**If you cannot avoid seeing certain things, then try facing them head-on.** Start by touching them. If Y had only looked at her husband's things without touching them, she would never have been able to see them as anything other than toys. Once she held it in her hand, however, the object became real. A figurine, for example, was no longer an anonymous samurai but the great leader Takeda Shingen. This alone can reduce aversion to such objects by half.

There may be some things, however, that you simply cannot bear to touch, and in such cases, you don't need to force yourself. For some people, photos of insects or a diorama of a zombie movie may just be too grotesque. If you know with a single glance that you have an innate aversion to something, don't torture yourself with it. In addition, never touch something that another person considers either very precious or very private without his or her permission. **You don't have to make yourself like someone else's things. It's enough just to be able to accept them.**

While they do not belong to you, things that belong to the rest of your family are part of the home in which you live. From the perspective of the larger entity that is your home, your things and everyone else's things are all equally its children. This is a very important point to understand. Although your family lives under the same roof, the rule is that each person should have his or her own personal space. If people have a clearly defined area in which they are free to do as they want, they will automatically at least keep their things from encroaching on anyone else's space. If personal space is not clearly delineated in this way, people will lose track of the limitations of the storage spaces and their things will accumulate, making it hard for both people and things to enjoy the home.

Another rule is that once the space has been divided, we should ignore how the others use their own space. Earlier in this book I suggested that you create your own personal power spot in your home; your family members also need their own power spots. And if others in the family tidy even a little bit, praise, don't criticize them. Tidying is naturally contagious, but if you try to force it on someone else, you'll only be met with harsh resistance. Like Aesop's fable about the north wind and the sun, it is far more effective to be like the sun.

# Don't force people to tidy if they don't want to

To tell the truth, I've been told that one person I helped tidy as part of a TV programme rebounded spectacularly afterward. Although the programme differed from my regular lessons, still, this was the first person I had helped complete the tidying process who had ever rebounded. I was not only sorry but so shocked that it took me a while to recover.

Thanks to this, however, I realized that I had been guilty of pride. I had been so certain that no one who took lessons from me, no matter how messy their house, could ever rebound. It also hit me that I had assumed that everyone in the world would be happy to live in a neat and tidy home. I later learned that the person concerned was quite happy living in a cluttered space.

'How can I make my family tidy up?' This is one of the most common questions I receive. But when I interview those who ask and meet their families, there's usually very little I can do to help because the family members don't have a strong urge to change. One of my favourite books is *The Thrilling Art of Not Discarding!* by Shinobu Machida (published by Gakuyosha Publishing Co., Ltd). Machida, a naturalist, likes to collect chocolate and *natto* (fermented soybean) packages and has thousands of each. He declares, 'I don't like spacious homes that feel like they haven't been lived in,' and goes on to extol the virtue of *not* discarding. What brings him joy is the space he lives in right now, which is filled with things.

Naturally, the kind of living space that brings a person joy depends on that particular individual's values. We can't change others. And we should never force someone else to tidy. **Only when we accept unconditionally people whose values differ from our own can we really say that we have finished tidying.**

When I lived with my family, I never once succeeded in making our house match my image of the ideal lifestyle. I don't know how many times I sighed at the sight of my siblings' rooms, which had far more stuff than mine, or the bathroom sink area, which was always a mess within mere hours of tidying it. Although I'm ashamed to admit it, I was arrogantly convinced that my family couldn't possibly be getting any joy out of life while living in such a state. In fact, people who choose to live like this are often quite happy with their lives. Feeling sorry for them was a waste of my energy.

Through this experience, I realized that when I start judging others, it's usually because something in my own life needs to be put in order, whether it's my room or some job that I've been putting off. This applies not just to me but to almost everyone who feels this way, whether they are currently in the midst of tidying or have already finished. When things that belong to others bother you, the trick is to stay on track and focus on tidying your own space. **When you have truly finished tidying, you'll see what you want or absolutely must do next, so you really don't have time to waste on complaining about others**. While I have pretty much finished the physical task of tidying up, this is an issue that I, too, am still working on.

What should you do if you've finished tidying your space completely but your family's mess still irritates you? To help reduce your feelings of frustration, I recommend applying yourself to cleaning.

There are only three steps involved in daily tidying: returning things to their proper place, thanking them every time you use them and taking good care of them. After that comes cleaning. The point is to clean thoroughly, starting with your own personal space. Once you've cleaned it to the point where you can keep it that way, then you can tackle communal spaces such as the entrance hall and the bathroom.

Instead of expecting others to tidy, devote all your attention to confronting the things in your house. It is this process that helps eliminate irritation. As you work away, your house will become visibly cleaner, and before you know it, you will be feeling calm and relieved.

The next step is how to respond to your family if,

inspired by how happy you look, they begin to show an interest in tidying themselves. The time to offer your assistance is when you see this interest emerge. But remember: you're only offering to help, not to critique their joy criteria or to make decisions for them. It's a lot of work to gather all your things together in one spot and carry out all the bags. The reason many people can't get started even when the desire arises is because it seems like such a huge task. Offering practical, physical support is an effective way to encourage people to take that first step.

Of course, if they want to do it on their own, don't insist on helping. And if they start asking questions such as, 'Do you think it's okay to get rid of this?' respond with a supportive, 'Sure, it'll be fine.'

## Teach your children how to fold

Once you have completely finished your tidying, one useful thing you can teach those who have avoided tidying thus far is how to fold. Mastering how to fold clothes can actually determine whether or not a person will stay motivated to carry on tidying.

While the ability to identify something you love by holding it in your hand can only be honed through experience, folding is a skill that can be acquired much faster if someone teaches you how. This is true for children learning to tidy as well.

'My kids make such a mess all the time. It drives me nuts . . .' Clients who say things like this are usually trying to teach their children to put away their toys as the first step in encouraging them to tidy, but this is the wrong place to start. Toys are very hard to categorize because there is so much variety and they are made of such a vast range of materials. This makes storing them quite complex. Nor do children play with the same toys every day or in the same way. Thus, tidying toys is too advanced for beginners.

Clothes, on the other hand, can be categorized relatively easily, and we wear pretty much the same types every day. Once children learn how to fold, it's easy for them to put clothes away in their proper place. This makes it the easiest category for training children. Best of all, when you teach them to express gratitude to their clothes as they fold them, you are teaching them not just the need to put things away after using them, but the very essence of tidying. For this reason, folding is the one essential tidying skill for both adults and children.

'I tried folding with my family and we all had a great time!' This is the most frequent response to my TV demonstrations on how to fold. Folding is great. It fosters communication and helps tidy up your house to boot. Whether or not your family will catch the tidying bug is really up to you, so I hope you will have fun folding clothes together.

# Even if you fail, don't worry – your house won't blow up

Recently, I started learning how to bake bread. One of my clients runs a café and the bread she serves is scrumptious. I was just wishing that I could make bread like that when I found out that she gives lessons. I signed up right away.

Her classes, which remind me of science experiments, are fascinating. After learning the basics of how to make bread, we alter different parts of the recipe, such as the rising time, and compare the results. This means we get to eat a lot of delicious bread. The teacher explains the changes that occur in the different ingredients and the reason they result in different flavours and textures so that we can understand how the process works. We pick the varieties we like best among the various experiments, try reproducing them at home and then share what we learn at the next lesson with feedback from the teacher. Having spent my life immersed in tidying without ever baking bread, I confess that I was nervous about every little thing.

One day, the other students and I were firing off our questions and concerns.

'It says here that when adding pureed vegetables, the amount should be no more than 20 per cent, but I want a really carroty bread. Is it okay to add a little more?'

'I can't tell when to stop kneading.'

'I always let it rise too long.'

Our teacher responded patiently to all our questions. When she had finished, she smiled. 'Don't worry,' she said. 'It's not going to blow up or anything!'

These words were a revelation. I had set the standard so high that I was petrified of failure even before I got started. Bread is made by combining and baking wheat, water, and yeast. If you follow the basic rules, fresh baked bread is almost always delicious, and even if you make a mistake, it won't be a major disaster. Instead of getting so uptight about it, I could just approach bread baking like any other type of cooking. The teacher was encouraging us to enjoy experimenting so that we could find our own personal favourites. After all, each person will have his or her own preferences concerning the type of flour, baking time, and so on.

Tidying is the same. During the question period after my lessons, many people raise their hands.

'There's a closet in the hallway. I keep my winter coats and scarves there where I can grab them easily on my way out. But should I stop doing that because it means my clothes storage is in more than one place?'

My response is to go ahead and keep them in the hall. These clothes have obviously been identified as the separate category of 'things to put on before leaving the house' and therefore clothes storage is by no means scattered.

'You said not to let our families see what we dispose of, but when I'm tidying with my husband, he tells me what doesn't suit me or points out that I never use certain things. I find his advice really helpful, and it's much more fun doing it together. But should I stop so that I can commune with my things silently?'

Again, my response is to go ahead and continue. As long as she doesn't follow any advice that doesn't bring joy, it's not a problem. The only thing to keep in mind is this: no matter how you go about deciding what to get rid of, in the end it is you alone who bears responsibility for that choice.

'I just can't do it!' a client recently exclaimed. 'I can fold my socks and underwear, but when it comes to cardigans and jumpers, forget it. I just use hangers. Is there any other way to do this?' Hanging them is perfectly fine. Because it takes up more space, however, you may need to compensate by using thinner hangers if you have a lot of things to hang.

From this you can see that all of my clients find their own unique ways of tidying, yet because they want to do it 'right', they are constantly afraid of failing. Let me assure you, it's going to be okay. Even if you make a mistake, your house isn't going to blow up. The first step is to get rid of any assumptions you may have and follow the basic rules of tidying. Once you have done that, then you will enjoy tidying far more if you adjust the finer points to suit your own sense of joy. This will also allow you to finish your tidying festival in a shorter time.

Are you enjoying your tidying festival? Or has tidying itself become your goal, making it seem like a penance so that the very thought of tidying is stressful? Are you beginning to feel that you won't be able to go on to anything else until you finish tidying up? When I meet people who feel this way, it reminds me of myself as a high school student when I was so obsessed with tidying that I had a nervous breakdown.

If this is how you feel, please give yourself a break. Stop tidying and focus instead on cherishing the things you have. Pause to say 'thank you' to the clothes you are wearing, to your pen or computer, your dishes and quilts, the bath and the kitchen. Without exception, the things in your home long to make you happy. Once you see that they are there to protect and support you, once you realize that you have enough even now, then you can resume tidying.

**Those who enjoy their tidying marathon win.** As long as you acquire a firm grasp of the basics, then go ahead and make your own decisions, guided by what brings you joy. My bread making at this point still has a long way to go. I frequently forget to put in an ingredient, knead it too long or fall asleep while it's rising. But I'm having fun, so I know that it's bound to work out in the end.

# Things that spark joy soak up precious memories

As I continued to teach clients how to tidy, people began to call me 'teacher'. I long ago reached the point where I had just the right amount of possessions in my life, and, having stayed true to my sense of joy and practised the rules of my trade, my wardrobe never overflows with clothes, nor do books end up stacked on my floor. Of course, I buy new clothes and other things, but I also let go of those that have served their purpose. Consequently, I never feel inundated with things, and, confident that I can care for them well, I feel very good about my relationship to the things I own. Yet, until recently, I felt that something was still missing. There seemed to be something my clients had discovered through tidying that I had yet to find.

Then, not long ago, I went cherry blossom viewing with my family for the first time in fifteen years. I had reached a bit of a block in my work and suddenly decided to call them up and invite them to go. We didn't go anywhere special, just to a little park near my house. The fact that it's not well known actually makes it a great place for cherry blossom viewing. The trees were in full bloom, but no one else stopped to spread out a picnic blanket underneath, so we had them all to ourselves.

Despite the sudden notice, my mother had prepared a picnic lunch, and my sister and I behaved like excited little girls. Unwrapping and opening the lunch box, we found nori-wrapped *onigiri* stuffed with pickled plum and grilled salmon, fried chicken, a sweet potato dish, and red and yellow cherry tomatoes. While the menu was limited, it was packed beautifully and obviously with a loving care that touched my heart. The sight of the neatly arranged contents activated the tidying freak in me, and I couldn't help comparing it to the perfect example of a well-organized drawer.

But that was not all. My mother opened another package to reveal a bottle of pink-hued amazake, a beverage made from sweet fermented rice, and small pink glasses with a cherry blossom pattern. When filled with the pink amazake, it looked like cherry blossoms were blooming in our glasses. 'How beautiful!' The blossoms I viewed that day with my family were the best I had ever seen.

When I returned home, something about my apartment seemed different. Nothing had actually changed since I left it the day before. It was still the place I loved filled with all the things that bring me joy, each resting comfortably where it belonged. At that moment, an image of the blossom-patterned glasses we had used that afternoon rose in my mind. And finally I knew. The glasses that my mother had chosen showed me the precious piece I had been missing. **I want to live my life in such a way that it colours my things with memories.**

The glasses were an expression of my mother's love and affection, chosen out of her desire to make that day special for us, even just a little. I had seen those glasses in our house many times and had always thought they were pretty, but they had been transformed into 'those special cups that my mother filled with amazake when we went to view the blossoms'. I realized that the value of things with which I have spent precious hours alone cannot compare with the value of things that bear precious memories of time spent with other people.

My favourite clothes and shoes are special, and I wear them constantly, but they can't compete with things that have been steeped in memories of the people I love. I realized that what I had really longed for was just to be with my family. Compared to the amount of time I spent with my possessions, myself, and my work, I had spent far less time interacting with my loved ones. Of course, I will still continue to value my time alone. But the purpose of it is to nurture me so that I can enjoy an even more fulfilling time with my loved ones, so that I can contribute even more to the happiness of the others around me.

If the glasses had been plain and ordinary, I would still have remembered the beverage my mother had brought, but I doubt that I would have remembered the glasses. Objects that have been steeped in memories carry a much clearer imprint of special times. Objects steeped in memories keep the past crystal clear within our minds. And objects that bring us joy have even greater capacity to soak up our memories. When those glasses finally break, as some day they must, when they have finished their job and the time to thank them and bid them farewell finally comes, I know they will have left the memory of our blossom-viewing picnic etched forever in my heart.

**Our things form a part of us, and when they're gone, they leave behind them eternal memories.**

As long as I face my belongings sincerely and keep only those that I love, as long as I cherish them while they are with me and consciously seek to make my time with them as precious as possible, every day will be filled with warmth and joy. This knowledge makes my heart feel so much lighter.

Therefore, I urge you once again: finish putting your things in order as soon as you can, so that you can spend the rest of your life surrounded by the people and things that you love most.

# Epilogue

At the age of fifteen or so, having awakened to the call of tidying, I spent every day tidying not just my own room but virtually every space in our home, from my siblings' rooms to the kitchen, the living room and the bathroom. Because I tell this story everywhere I go, many people assume that our house must have become very tidy, but I'm afraid that this was far from the case. Even after I published my first book, nothing changed. Then one day, I received the following email.

'Dear KonMari, Please teach me how to tidy.'

I always give priority to clients who have reserved a lesson, but when I saw the sender, I immediately decided to forgo a planned vacation and schedule him in.

The request for tidying lessons was from, of all people, my father.

He was now using the room that used to be mine, a six-tatami-mat (nine by twelve-foot) room with a single wardrobe and a built-in bookcase. It was small, with only a bed and a little writing desk, but for me, it was like paradise. I kept it very clean, wiping the floor every night before going to bed.

When I went home, however, I found it completely changed. The first thing I saw upon opening the door was a clothing rack standing right in front of the wardrobe, completely blocking one of its doors. A cardboard box filled with emergency food rations to be used in the event of a disaster sat on the floor, and beside it was a set of two large plastic drawers filled with surplus cleaning supplies and other paraphernalia. A pile of magazines towered in front of the built-in bookcase, and, worst of all, a new digital television had been plunked on top of the old analogue TV, in a bold TV-on-TV arrangement.

Just to make sure there's no misunderstanding, my father actually enjoys cleaning and interior decorating and is usually quite conscientious about keeping things neat. However, the one thing he just can't bring himself to do is to discard. He announced to my mother that he wouldn't dispose of any of his clothes until he died, and for ten years he had steadfastly resisted my urgings to reduce. Only after he became so busy at work that he no longer had time to tidy daily was he forced to admit that his room was a disaster site, and he finally made up his mind to do something about it.

Thus began my father's tidying lessons. As usual, we started by gathering all his clothes in one place, and there seemed to be no end of these. There were reams of clothes with the tags still on, countless pairs of underwear still in their plastic wrappers, never-worn jackets he had forgotten even existed, masses of polo shirts of exactly the same design. This inspired the typical reaction: 'Do I really have this much stuff?!?' We then moved on to picking up each item and selecting only those that sparked joy. It gave me a strange feeling to watch my father confronting his possessions one by one and making decisions. Somewhat tentatively, he announced, 'This brings me joy,' 'For this one, I'm grateful,' and 'I'm sorry I couldn't use you.' Over the next two days we went through his things in the correct order of clothes, books, papers, *komono* and sentimental items. After completely sorting his things and getting rid of twenty bags of stuff, we tackled the bathroom and communal spaces. Then we finished off with a lesson on storage.

At the end, my father's room looked like a completely different and very joyful world. Everything but his bed and the TV had been put away, and the wood flooring was once again visible. The bookcase held only books and CDs that he loved, and a shelf, now virtually empty, held a pottery ornament my younger sister had made in high school and figurines of a jazz band that he had bought by mail order. As a finishing touch, he hung a painting that had until now been stuck in the wardrobe, and the whole room seemed bright and attractive, like a model home interior.

'I kept telling myself I would get to this sometime; that I would do it next week for sure,' my father said. 'I'm just so relieved that I finally did it. When you get down to business, it's amazing what a transformation can take place in just two days.' Hearing the satisfaction in his voice, I realized that this had been a great way to show him my love. Even someone like my father, who had avoided tidying for a whole decade, can do it very quickly once they set their mind to it and can witness the dramatic impact it has on their life.

Afterword:

# Preparing for the next stage of your life

'I had read about how to tidy up completely, but I never got started because it seemed like so much work . . . When I finally committed myself, it was even more work than I had expected. I had so much stuff, and I was really busy at work. It took me a whole year. I spent all my holidays tidying . . . Then, just the other day, I reached the end. I finished my photos and all the pending items in one go . . . I feel like I've been reborn. Wherever I look, all I see are things that spark joy. I feel a tenderness for everything in my life and am just so thankful!'

When I receive letters like this, my mind fills with images of the sender's future as they move on to the next stage of their lives. Living mindfully in a beautiful space, they will now be able to give up any habits they've always

275

wanted to quit, to see clearly what they really want to achieve and to do what it takes to get there.

To put your house in order is to put your life in order and prepare for the next step. Once you have dealt properly with the current phase of your life, the next will come to you naturally. I put my things in order during my university years. Since then, I feel I have been able to greet each new event in my life and deal with whatever is needed.

For me, the most recent stage began in the spring of 2014 when I got married. Starting my own family is helping me to see things from a new perspective. For one thing, I am learning that unspoken family rules differ from one household to another, and that storage methods I had assumed were obvious need to be properly shared and explained. When I was single, my house contained only my own things, but now they share space with my husband's things. And I want to take as good care of his things as I do of my own.

 With that thought in mind, we recently spent some time as a couple tidying up. We didn't need to do a full-out tidying campaign because, due to the nature of my work, I own only the bare minimum, and my husband's lifestyle is so compact that his belongings filled only four cardboard boxes when he moved in. Instead, we had a lesson in folding and storing clothes.

I explained how to fold each type, how to store folded things upright and how to hang things so that they rise to the right. We chatted away as we worked. Until then, I had believed that it was best for each individual to work separately on tidying his or her own things, but from this experience, I realized that it can actually be helpful to have some time as a family to commune with our possessions. The process of tidying seems to deepen the relationships not only between our things and our home but also between our things and ourselves and between ourselves and our family.

As I reflected on the nature of these relationships, it occurred to me that Japanese people have treated material things with special care since ancient times. The concept of *yaoyorozu no kami*, literally, '800,000 gods', is an example. The Japanese believed that gods resided not only in natural phenomena such as the sea and the land but also in the cooking stove and even in each individual grain of rice, and therefore they treated all of them with reverence. During the Edo period of 1603–1868, Japan appears to have had a well-organized and thorough recycling system to ensure that nothing was wasted. The idea that everything is imbued with spirit would seem to be engraved in the Japanese DNA.

There are three facets to the spirit that dwells in material things: the spirit of the materials from which the things are made, the spirit of the person who made them, and the spirit of the person who uses them. The spirit of the maker has an especially powerful impact on an object's personality. For example, this book you are reading is paper. But it is not just any old paper. It is paper that is instilled with my ardent wish that you will try tidying up and my longing to help those who want to live a life that sparks joy. The intensity of these feelings will continue to pervade the air even after you have closed this book.

Yet, in the end, it is the feelings of the person who uses an object, the way in which he or she treats it, that will determine what kind of aura it has (the Japanese is *kuki-kan*, literally, 'feeling of the air'). The light this book radiates, the presence it exudes, will depend on you and how you treat it, on whether you make use of it or just buy it and never read it. This is true for all things, not just this book: your mind determines the value of everything you own.

Recently, an expression that keeps coming to mind as I work with my clients is *mono no aware*. This Japanese term, which literally means 'pathos of things', describes the deep emotion that is evoked when we are touched by nature, art or the lives of others with an awareness of their transience. It also refers to the essence of things and our ability to feel that essence. As my clients proceed through the tidying process, I sense a change in the words they say, and in their facial expressions, as if they are sharpening their ability to feel *mono no aware*.

One of my clients, for example, gazed at a bicycle she had cherished and used for years, and then said, 'You know, this bike, I just realized that she's been like my partner in life.'

Another client told me with a smile, 'Even my cooking chopsticks seem incredibly dear to me now.' It is not only their feelings for material possessions that change. They are also able to slow down and physically savour the changing of the seasons, and they become much kinder to themselves and their families.

I believe that when we put our things in order and strengthen our bonds with what we own, we get back in touch with that delicate sensitivity to *mono no aware*. We rediscover our innate capacity to cherish the things in our lives and regain the awareness that our relationship with the material world is one of mutual support.

If you feel anxious all the time but are not sure why, try putting your things in order. Hold each thing you own in your hands and ask yourself whether or not it sparks joy. Then cherish the ones that you decide to keep, just as you cherish yourself, so that every day of your life will be filled with joy.

# Acknowledgements

My tidying journey began when I was fifteen. At one point, I thought I would be giving private tidying lessons my whole life, but along the way my approach to tidying changed. I now have two apprentices and have established a nationwide association to train tidying consultants around the country. In addition, *The Life-Changing Magic of Tidying* has been translated and published in more than thirty-five countries around the world. The response has far exceeded my expectations. I am not only elated but also totally amazed that the KonMari Method, which evolved from my manic obsession with tidying, is spreading around the world. I was even further astounded to find myself the subject of an article in the *New York Times* and to be receiving messages from people overseas. To share the KonMari Method, I hope to visit a range of countries and undertake an international tidying survey.

As I mentioned briefly, getting married has been a major change in my life. Thanks to my husband, who is simply too good at housework, I have even more time to devote to my passion. As a self-professed tidying freak, this keeps me both busy and happy.

In closing, let me take this opportunity to express my profound gratitude to the many people without whose collaboration and support this book would never have been possible. Thank you to my translator, Cathy Hirano; my American publishing team at Ten Speed Press/ Crown Publishing, especially Lisa Westmoreland, Daniel Wikey, Hannah Rahill, Aaron Wehner, David Drake, and Maya Mavjee; my agents Neil Gudovitz and Jun Hasebe; and my Japanese publishing team at Sunmark Publishing, particularly Nobutaka Ueki, Tomohiro Takahashi, Ichiro Takeda, and Shino Kobayashi.

I am also extremely grateful to each one of you who chose to pick up this book and read it. Thank you all so much.

Marie 'KonMari' Kondo

# Index